PRAISE FOR *GASLIGHTING*

"A succinct, useful self-help guide to responding to an all-too-common but under-discussed personality type."

—*Publishers Weekly*

"Sarkis clearly knows her material inside and out . . . this book will bring gaslighting victims and survivors out of the darkness and into the light, helping them heal."

—*New York Journal of Books*

"A fascinating and necessary study of rampant gaslighting and how to steer clear of being a victim."

—*Library Journal*, starred review

HEALING
FROM
TOXIC
RELATIONSHIPS

Also by Stephanie Moulton Sarkis, PhD

*Gaslighting: Recognize Manipulative and
Emotionally Abusive People—and Break Free*

*Executive Function Difficulties in Adults: 100 Ways to
Help Your Clients Live Productive and Happy Lives*

*Natural Relief for Adult ADHD: Complementary
Strategies for Increasing Focus, Attention, and
Motivation with or Without Medication*

Adult ADHD: A Guide for the Newly Diagnosed

*ADD and Your Money: A Guide to Personal Finance
for Adults with Attention Deficit Disorder*

*Making the Grade with ADD: A Student's Guide to
Succeeding in College with Attention Deficit Disorder*

*10 Simple Solutions to Adult ADD: How to Overcome
Chronic Distraction & Accomplish Your Goals*

HEALING FROM TOXIC RELATIONSHIPS

10 Essential Steps
to Recover from
Gaslighting, Narcissism,
and **Emotional Abuse**

By Stephanie Moulton Sarkis, PhD

hachette
BOOKS

New York

Copyright © 2022 by Sarkis Media LLC

Cover design by Terri Sirma
Cover copyright © 2022 by Hachette Book Group, Inc.

Hachette Go, an imprint of Hachette Books
Hachette Book Group
1290 Avenue of the Americas
New York, NY 10104
HachetteGo.com
Facebook.com/HachetteGo
Instagram.com/HachetteGo

First Edition: July 2022

Hachette Books is a division of Hachette Book Group, Inc.

The Hachette Go and Hachette Books name and logos are trademarks of Hachette Book Group, Inc.

The publisher is not responsible for websites (or their content) that are not owned by the publisher.

Print book interior design by Amy Quinn.

Library of Congress Cataloging-in-Publication Data

Names: Sarkis, Stephanie, author.
Title: Healing from toxic relationships : 10 essential steps to recover
   from gaslighting, narcissism, and emotional abuse / by Stephanie Moulton
   Sarkis, PhD.
Description: First edition. | New York : Hachette Go, [2022] | Includes
   bibliographical references and index.
Identifiers: LCCN 2022005911 | ISBN 9780306847257 (paperback) | ISBN
   9780306847240 (ebook)
Subjects: LCSH: Interpersonal conflict. | Interpersonal relations. |
   Manipulative behavior. | Narcissism. | Psychological abuse.
Classification: LCC BF637.I48 S27 2022 | DDC 158.2—dc23/eng/20220303
LC record available at https://lccn.loc.gov/2022005911

ISBNs: 978-0-306-84725-7 (trade paperback); 978-0-306-84724-0 (ebook)

Printed in Canada

FRI

10 9 8 7 6 5 4 3 2 1

To survivors of trauma—may you find hope on your journey to healing

CONTENTS

INTRODUCTION

WHEN HER MOTHER DRANK, JANE FELT THERE WAS NOTHING SHE could do to make her happy. Sometimes, Jane's mother would fly into rages where she told the children that they had ruined her life, and she wished they had never been born. Jane's mother especially seemed to hold contempt for Jane—tripping or hitting her, and then kicking her when she was on the ground. Jane's mother even ordered Jane's sister to kick her. Meanwhile, Jane's father would leave the house or go into another room and shut the door. "Just try not to upset your mother," he told Jane.

As an adult, Jane finds some sense of normalcy and even comfort in chaos. A healthy relationship seems boring to her. She has an exaggerated startle reaction, and when someone raises their voice or yells, she checks out and goes into a dissociative state. Jane compensates for feeling inadequate by throwing herself into her work. Some of her friends have called her a workaholic. She recently lost her job, and she has entered a downward spiral.

• • • • •

When Hasim was hired, his employer told him that he would be working with a close-knit team. "We're like family," his new boss assured him. Hasim quickly found out they were truly like family—a dysfunctional one. Hasim's coworker Sal takes credit for his work, including a project that

Hasim spent six months developing. Sal will say racial slurs to Hasim, just loud enough for him to hear. Hasim finally asked his other coworkers whether they'd ever had issues getting along with Sal. "Sal usually finds one target out of the group," his teammate Sarah said as the others nodded. "I just ignore him . . . but I guess that's easier when I'm not his chosen victim."

One day Sal openly criticized Hasim during a staff meeting. "You don't pull your weight around the office, Hasim," Sal told him. "But I'm not surprised. You're as lazy as we all expected."

Hasim had had enough. "You're bullying me, Sal," he said clearly. "And it's not just me. You've been harassing other people here, too." But when Hasim looked around for backup, his teammates were silent. Later, a coworker confided that he wasn't going to say anything because he didn't want to get on Sal's bad side again. Hasim went to his boss with documentation of Sal's behaviors, but his boss said that Sal was an "exemplary employee" and he had never known anyone to have issues with him. Now Hasim has a feeling of dread when he wakes up in the morning. Sal is now claiming that Hasim has harassed *him*. Hasim is hunting for other jobs.

· · · · ·

When Ken and Sabrina met in high school, one of the things that they bonded over was their "messed-up" families; their parents got into screaming matches on a nightly basis. Unknowingly, they followed their parents' example, and their own relationship was intense and full of conflict. Sometimes, their fights escalated into shoving. But they would always make up, and it felt as if they were stronger than ever—strong enough to continue their relationship long-distance in college. Both thought that they were so "passionate" because they were so in love. That was, until they went away to college, and Sabrina realized how much more at peace she felt when Ken wasn't around.

Ken seemed to sense Sabrina pulling away, and he would call and text her demanding to know where she was and who she was with. He also posted photos on social media with other girls at parties, looking like he was having the time of his life. Sabrina was seized with jealousy and started losing sleep. She felt that she was constantly checking his profile and her grades started slipping. Deciding it was time to end things, she texted him, "I can't do this anymore," and blocked his number, email, and social media accounts. That night, Ken showed up outside her apartment. At first she felt somewhat flattered, thinking of how much he must love her to do something like that. But then he started yelling from the parking lot, calling her terrible names. She kept her lights off and didn't respond. Now, every now and then Ken will text Sabrina from an unknown number, acting as if he's just "checking in." These texts always make Sabrina feel sick, and she wonders whether she'll ever really be able to relax again.

• • • • •

If you're reading this book, you can probably relate to Jane, Hasim, and Sabrina. Any relationship—whether it's with a romantic partner, a family member, a friend, or even a coworker—takes work. Even the closest relationships will have their ups and downs. But when there is competition, conflict, jealousy, resentment, hostility, abuse, and controlling behavior, it's a sign that a relationship has become toxic.

You may have recently ended a toxic relationship, or perhaps you're considering leaving one. Life in the aftermath of a toxic relationship can be a struggle. You may have left the relationship with wounds to your heart and your self-esteem. You might be feeling rage and betrayal. You may also be pretty mean to yourself, blaming yourself for things that are not your fault. You may be feeling stuck and unsure how to move on. It may be that you are exploring your options, but you aren't ready to completely end a toxic relationship, or you can't leave yet due to logistics or finances.

Perhaps you're not reading this book for yourself. You may be a clinician that works with clients who have survived domestic or intimate partner violence or are in dysfunctional families. You may care about or love someone who has experienced a toxic relationship. While you can't fix a person's situation for them, this book can give you ways to provide help and support.

Whatever your situation, I want you to know that how you're feeling is entirely normal—and it's within your power to break free. You can heal, and you will feel better.

How I Came to This Topic

I'm a clinician in private practice specializing in treating ADHD, anxiety, and narcissistic abuse. Because toxic people tend to target individuals with exactly these kinds of vulnerabilities, I tend to see more survivors of toxic relationships and abuse than other therapists do. I am a Florida Supreme Court certified family and circuit mediator and have seen firsthand how toxic relationships can play out in the legal system, particularly in custody disputes. Toxic people also tend to prolong legal battles instead of trying to settle them. Seasoned judges and attorneys usually recognize these signs immediately. However, some toxic people are so good at manipulation that even some mental health professionals don't see it.

Much as I've seen the damage that a toxic situation can do, I've also come to see certain patterns in toxic people's behavior, particularly the "idealize, devalue, and discard" cycle, emotional abuse, and gaslighting (all of which I'll describe in detail in Chapter 1). My last book, *Gaslighting: Recognize Manipulative and Emotionally Abusive People—and Break Free*, explored gaslighting in all its forms so that readers could identify harmful relationships and get out of them. In twenty years of private practice, I have seen an increase in clients reporting gaslighting behaviors in their partners, family, employers, and coworkers. The patterns of behavior they have experienced have a push-pull nature to them, where toxic people reel them in, get them hooked, and then abruptly push them away. Many clients will attend their first therapy appointment wondering whether they were the toxic person in the relationship—when the other person's behavior clearly qualifies as inappropriate and even dangerous. When *gaslighting* became a commonly used term, more clients began disclosing their experiences in therapy. In some cases, clients had been in a toxic relationship for years, attempting to leave and then getting sucked back in. It was only upon limiting or blocking contact with a toxic person that my clients were fully able to rebuild their lives. By having a name for the behavior they had endured, they were able to recognize it and ultimately separate themselves from it.

My book *Gaslighting* is mostly about identifying and extracting yourself from harmful relationships. This book picks up where that one left off to explore the aftermath—as well as what you can do to protect yourself, heal, and avoid toxic relationships in the future.

In This Book

First, a note: Throughout this book, I'll switch pronouns, using "he" or "him" and "she" or "her," or plurals to reflect that this information applies regardless of gender. People of any sex can be toxic, abusive, or manipulative. Although you will more often hear about toxic men, women can and do carry out these behaviors (though abuse from women is sometimes not seen as abuse or taken as seriously). Men who experience toxicity and abuse deserve support and healing, just as women do. Abuse can occur in LGBTQ+ relationships. One of my goals with this book is to correct those misunderstandings. I also hope to broaden recognition of toxic behavior beyond just romantic relationships. It can also happen in friendships, families, and professional relationships.

As you read this book, you may find yourself saying, "Well, that doesn't apply to me," or "My situation wasn't like that." It's important to know that while toxic relationships share some features, each is unique. This is not a one-size-fits-all kind of book. That said, I encourage you to read everything, even if you think a particular section might not apply to you. Toxic relationships and situations can be very complex and you may just find wisdom that will help you in an unexpected place.

Here's what you'll find in the chapters to come. In Chapter 1, "How Did We Get Here?," you will learn what defines a relationship as toxic. You will also discover whether the people around you are genuinely toxic. It can be tricky sometimes to know who is "okay" and who is not, especially if you grew up around emotionally unhealthy people. Knowing what a toxic relationship is or isn't can help you make educated decisions about who you allow into your life.

The best way to heal from toxic people is to block them from contacting you—including blocking their texts, phone calls, emails, and social media accounts. In Chapter 2, "Block Contact if You Can," you'll learn why going "radio silent" sometimes is the only way to gain back your life. You will also learn how to navigate contact with someone with whom you can't entirely stop contact, such as the parent of your children or someone in your workplace.

In Chapter 3, "(For)get Closure," you will learn that you may not receive any type of closure or finality after you end interactions with an unhealthy person. It is up to *you* to create closure, but it can be daunting and may even seem impossible at times. Keep in mind that getting closure in a traditional sense is not necessarily required to experience healing and an emotionally healthy life.

You may have experienced anger and even rage toward yourself for getting involved with a toxic person or situation. In Chapter 4, "Forgive Yourself," you'll discover how often people have no way of knowing in the beginning that a person is toxic. Part of healing is being open to the fact that you did nothing wrong while you were with a toxic person—even if the person repeatedly told you that everything was your fault. Letting go and forgiving yourself is an essential step toward healing.

In Chapter 5, "Establish Boundaries," you will learn healthy ways to protect yourself emotionally from toxic people. Healthy boundaries include being spoken to respectfully, having your belongings treated with care and your pets treated well, and feeling safe in your environment. Setting boundaries, such as how you expect to be treated, can take practice. Toxic people try to undermine and ignore your boundaries. In this chapter, you will learn how to enforce them.

No one gets through healing alone, and talking with a mental health professional (MHP) can help you sort out your feelings and guide you through your journey of healing. In Chapter 6, "Talk to a Professional," you will learn about the different types of MHPs and types of therapy they can provide, including cognitive-behavioral therapy and solution-focused therapy. You will also discover how to tell whether an MHP is a good fit for you.

In Chapter 7, "Practice Self-Care," you will discover why it is essential to take excellent care of yourself and practice self-compassion during your healing. That includes taking time for enjoyable activities and practicing good sleep habits. When you take care of yourself, it is easier to deal with the ups and downs of healing from a toxic relationship. When you treat yourself well, you set the tone for how others should treat you.

You may think that you are surviving the aftermath of a toxic relationship all on your own. That is one of the worst things about a toxic relationship—the feeling of isolation that is a product of abuse. Narcissists and other toxic people don't want you to maintain relationships and friendships with others because your support system means they have less control over you. Part of healing is reconnecting with healthy friends and family and also forming new connections with others. Discover how to best "reintroduce" yourself to people you care about in Chapter 8, "Reconnect."

After removing yourself from a toxic situation, you may experience an overwhelming feeling of loss. It's a loss that you may have already started grieving while you were in a toxic relationship. In Chapter 9, "Grieve," you will learn how grieving helps you understand what you experienced and how feeling "out of control" is part of the process. You will also learn how the grief you experience about a toxic relationship can be complicated, and you may feel multiple emotions at once. You will eventually come out on the other side of grief—and this chapter helps you through it.

One of the most important but least talked about parts of healing from a toxic relationship is devoting some of your time to helping others. In Chapter 10, "Volunteer," you will learn how being altruistic, or helping others, helps you. Volunteering provides an opportunity to connect with others and focus on a common positive goal. You will learn how to determine whether an organization is healthy, and if you feel called to do so, how to advocate for others who have experienced toxic relationships.

In Chapter 11, "Prevent," you will learn how to take the information you gained from the toxic relationship and use it to identify unhealthy people and situations. You may be finely tuned to people's issues after you exit a toxic relationship. Learn the difference between fear and intuition that you may experience when interacting with others. Discover the red flags that let you know that a person or situation is unhealthy. You can go on to have a fulfilling life and healthy relationships.

In this book, the chapters start from a broader view of toxic relationships and continue to more specific ways you can heal from abuse. While I recommend that you read all the chapters, it is okay if you read them out of order. Each chapter provides information on an integral part of healing. Throughout the chapters, you will find people's stories of their experiences, "check-ins," and activities that can help you through the healing process. For example, you'll learn how journaling can be an effective way of processing what you have been through and seeing how far you've come in your healing process. If you don't already have a journal or note-taking app, now would be a good time to get one. You'll also learn how being active can help with symptoms of anxiety, depression, and grief, and how practicing good sleep habits can help you think more clearly and make healthier decisions.

As you read this book, have it guide you in healing and rebuilding a new life. You've already taken the first step. Let's go on to the next—taking a step back to better understand toxic relationships and why they form.

1

HOW DID WE GET HERE?

What a Toxic Relationship Looks Like and
How to Identify Toxic People

NOBODY EXPECTS TO BE INVOLVED IN A TOXIC RELATIONSHIP. THESE DY-
namics can form quickly and without any signs of potential danger.
For instance, you may have been hired by someone who seemed to have
your best interests in mind yet who later turned out to play favorites,
or a partner may have showered you with affection in the beginning of
a relationship, but then their behavior became increasingly abusive. Or
you might have grown up with unhealthy family dynamics—say, a parent
who was loving and caring when she wasn't drinking, or a sibling who
was the favored child in your family, while you struggled to be accepted.
These relationships can take different forms, and in some of the sneakiest
ones, you don't realize it's abusive until you have been experiencing toxic
behavior for months or even years.

Is This Relationship Really Toxic?

You may be saying, "I already know what a toxic relationship is; that's
why I'm reading this book." On the other hand, you might not be sure if
what you're experiencing is truly problematic. So, ask yourself how many
of these statements apply to you and your relationship:

1. Since I have known this person, I have had more physical ailments—at least some of which can be attributed to stress or have been exacerbated by it.
2. Trusted friends and family have told me that this person is not healthy for me to be around.
3. I am belittled through this person's words and actions.
4. My interactions with this person have put me in a constant state of emotional turmoil.
5. I no longer trust my judgment.
6. I put others' needs above my own.
7. I blame myself for things that are not my fault.
8. I feel that I am a shadow of who I used to be.
9. I feel I am never good enough.
10. My work has been sabotaged and/or my devices have been hacked.
11. I spend more time Googling about the situation than taking steps to change it.
12. This person has turned others against me, such as my coworkers, friends, and family.
13. This person tells me that I am crazy and I will never find someone to love me.
14. This person tells me mean things that he claims my family and friends have said about me.
15. This person tells me that a lot of people know that I am crazy.
16. I am afraid to walk away from this situation.
17. This person has shoved/hit/slapped me or blocked me from being able to leave.
18. I feel I have no right to exist, or that I am "less than."
19. I engage in self-harm behaviors.
20. I have thought about suicide because of the way this person makes me feel.

If you agreed with even one of these statements, you might be in a toxic relationship. The more items you agreed with, the greater the chances.

Simply put, a toxic relationship is one where there is manipulation, gaslighting (see page 12), and abuse. It is a relationship that is damaging to you—mentally, emotionally, or even physically—and that seems to turn you into someone you no longer recognize. You consider yourself to be a reasonable person—at least you felt like one before you got into this relationship. Now, you might feel like a shell of your former self. Toxic people are like energy vampires. Simply being around them can leave you feeling like an empty husk of a person.

An important note: you may be thinking, *Well, my situation isn't that bad; I've heard of other people experiencing much worse.* Please know that there are many signs of toxic and abusive relationships; you don't have to check all the items in the previous list. And toxic situations usually aren't obviously unhealthy at first; these dynamics can develop over time, often so slowly that it can be hard to realize what's happening. See "Is It Abuse?" on page 9 for more on this.

It's common for people who display toxic behaviors to also have narcissistic tendencies, and in this book I will occasionally refer to a toxic person as a narcissist. These are people who tend to not take responsibility for their behavior, feel that they should be afforded special exceptions or rules, behave as if others are beneath them, and have self-focused behaviors. They tend to think of people in terms of what they can get from them. You may feel that a narcissist is showing you empathy, but the feelings you are seeing are most likely displays of *cognitive empathy*, meaning she has no real feelings behind those words and is just saying things to get you to think she cares. You may have heard of *narcissistic personality disorder (NPD)*. People may have signs of *narcissism* but not necessarily qualify for an NPD diagnosis. Think of narcissism as existing on a spectrum—on one end, narcissistic traits may just show up when someone is stressed. On the other end, a cluster of narcissistic symptoms impact a person's day-to-day functioning and ability to form healthy relationships. (To be clear, you can have a toxic relationship with someone who doesn't have narcissistic traits.)

Other common signs of a toxic relationship or situation include the following:

- Pathological lying
- Complaining about your or others' behavior but refusing any feedback
- Portraying herself as the victim in all her relationships
- Push-pull behaviors—swinging between "punishing" and "rewarding" you
- Pitting you against other people, or pitting children against one another
- Refusal to respect boundaries
- Period of intense anger followed by "nice" behavior
- Harassment and stalking
- Threatening to bankrupt you via the legal system
- Abandonment, or threatening to abandon you
- Yelling or raising their voice in a place where you have no exit, such as a car
- Leaving you stranded away from home
- Encouraging you to hurt yourself
- Blaming you for their behavior
- Saying cruel things and then insisting that they were just "joking"
- Undermining you
- Any kind of physical abuse, including blocking you from leaving
- Abuse toward children and pets
- Going through or hiding your belongings
- Accessing your home without your permission when you are out of town
- Refusing to talk about their behavior toward you
- Hacking into your electronic devices
- Telling you people have said mean or other unfavorable things about you
- Refusal to take responsibility for behavior
- Ruining your reputation with others
- Signing documents with your name, without your permission
- Stealing from you, including using your credit card without your permission or opening credit cards and accounts in your name

- Forcing you to quit your job so you can stay home
- Blaming you for defending yourself
- Forcing you to work
- Threatening to have you deported
- Taking your passport or other legal documents

In a Romantic Partnership

- Chronic infidelity
- Speaking poorly about their exes or bringing them up often
- Forcing you into sexual activity
- Rape, including having sex with you while you are sleeping or otherwise not able to give consent

In Family Relationships

- Forcing or guilting you into caretaking duties for an older or sick family member
- Threatening to disown you
- Flirting with or attempting to pick up your partner or spouse
- Coming over unexpectedly if it is not an accepted family practice

In the Workplace

- Taking credit for your work
- Changing deadlines frequently or drastically and not notifying you
- Giving you a poor performance review with no evidence
- Refusing to give you breaks during the workday
- Forcing you to disclose why you are taking a sick day
- Telling coworkers about health issues that you disclosed to your boss in confidence
- Refusing to pay you or issue correct tax documents
- Threatening to fire you over small mistakes
- Telling you to falsify documents

Any of these behaviors is cause for concern, and if you don't already work with a therapist or other mental health professional, I recommend that you meet with one to discuss your concerns. (In Chapter 6, we'll cover mental health professionals in depth—who they are, how they work, and how to connect with one.)

The Three Stages of a Toxic Relationship

In addition to the behaviors I just listed, there's another way to identify a toxic relationship: by its three characteristic stages—idealization, devaluing, and discard. The stages progress in that specific order. Let's take a closer look.

Toxic people are very persuasive and tend to look good on paper. When you met this person, you probably thought he had his act together. For example, a new boyfriend may have *love-bombed* you initially by telling you that he had never met anyone like you, putting you on a pedestal and showering you with gifts. Your boss might have told you that you are the smartest employee in the company. Your sibling told his friends, in front of you, that he would be totally lost without you. Your friend told you that you are the only friend she needs. This is the *idealizing* stage of a toxic relationship. The toxic person seemingly views you as perfect. However, that's not how he truly feels.

A narcissist needs a "supply," or a way to get his ego fed—someone who will tell him how wonderful he is, dote on him, and continually give him attention so he can mask deep-seated feelings of insecurity. The love-bombing is a ploy to keep you around: Because this person is telling you everything you want to hear, you are more likely to get into a relationship or continue contact. This is different than the early days of a new relationship where things are exciting and fresh. Love-bombing during the idealization stage is intense and seems too good to be true. Be very wary if someone is moving too quickly and trying to get you isolated or claim you as "their own." You may find that you have so much in common with this person—so much that it is eerie. However, he is just reflecting your behavior back to you to make you feel that you are truly heard and seen. He may ask you if you are fully in the relationship yet. Once they get that statement of commitment from you, devaluing begins.

Devaluing is a slow slippery slope. First, the toxic person might make comments under her breath—remarks about your appearance or behavior. Then, she may start to make blatant comments, even criticizing you in front of other people. The toxic person starts picking on things you can't change, such as your height or features of your body. Where you once could do no wrong, now you can do no right. You are embarrassed and ashamed. You start to blame yourself. How could this person who treated you like royalty now think that you are terrible?

You notice that she has a "mask" she wears in public. Everyone you know adores her, or at least thinks she's an okay person. However, when she gets angry, it's like her face completely changes. When she is caught cheating, instead of showing remorse, she blames you or denies it. She tells you what you saw or heard isn't real and that you must be going crazy.

Every once in a while, the toxic person will be very nice to you. Sometimes, it is after a fight (though she never apologizes for her behavior); sometimes, it seems to occur for no reason at all. This type of back-and-forth behavior is called *intermittent reinforcement*. When you don't know when the "good" version of the toxic person will appear, you tend to stick around longer. The lows are very low, but the highs are extraordinarily high. Our brain gets addicted to this unpredictability—making it very hard to leave the relationship. As an empathic person, you may blame yourself for this change. (Feeling responsible is normal, but I want you to know that this change is *not* your fault.) The toxic person may have told you that she acted out because of something you did. This push-pull of a toxic relationship results in trauma bonding, which you will learn more about later in this chapter.

The *discarding* phase of a toxic relationship happens when you are quickly dropped. The discard is as sudden and intense as the idealizing at the beginning of the relationship. You suffer two losses—the person you thought you knew doesn't exist, and the person he turned into is an absolute shock.

The discard is swift and brutal, and often makes no sense. The discard is sometimes preceded by rage. You somehow caused the person to have a *narcissistic injury*, or an event that threatens his ego. It could be that you didn't "obey" him, you caught him in deceitful behavior, he knows you are catching on to who he really is, or you brought up that his behavior concerned you. What you did could be so insignificant you may take a considerable amount of time trying to figure out what you did to set him off. Remember, you didn't do anything wrong.

Toxic people often have an issue with *object constancy*—which is the formal term for our ability to believe a relationship is stable even during conflicts or difficulties. A healthy person loves someone and also accepts that her partner or friend will do things that upset her sometimes. A healthy person also understands that it is her responsibility to respectfully address those issues. A narcissist has a "scorched earth" policy where he will end a relationship in a shocking and ugly way.

> "Once he knew I was committed to him, the devaluing happened quickly. The discard was cold and cruel. He was acting like he never had feelings for me. It was like he turned into a different person. His eyes looked cold and unfeeling."
>
> —Aisha, 32

Hoovering

After discarding you, a toxic person might "bench" you, giving you bread crumbs of attention to keep you around. When a toxic person thinks she is losing you, she will *hoover* you, or try to suck you back into the relationship. Once a toxic person feels she has "punished" you enough, she isn't getting enough attention, or you may be useful to her, she may contact you. Sometimes, she will leave a cryptic text to tempt you to answer back, or she will leave a voicemail acting as though the two of you are still on good terms.

It is normal to assume that the toxic person may have changed. We tend to expect some degree of change when people have behaved badly. However, in most cases, a toxic person is still up to the same tricks as before. She may just want to get confirmation that you are willing to answer her message. People tend to leave and return to toxic relationships multiple times before they leave for good.

Just like the three stages, hoovering can be easy to identify when you know the signs. They may tell you they miss you—but they rarely apologize for their behavior. If you ask for an apology, you might see their attitude go immediately from friendly to aggressive. The toxic person will also tell you anything to get you back. She will promise you that things will be different or offer exactly what she thinks it takes to get you back on her side. For instance, an ex might tell you he is finally ready to get married and have children; your mother could say that she will start attending a 12-step program for alcohol addiction; or your boss may offer you a raise if you stay. However, when you get back into the relationship, those plans have disappeared. When you bring it up, the person avoids the question or says that he is rethinking those promises because of something you did. This behavior of promising you the future you have wanted and then taking it away is called *future faking*. The toxicity just gets worse. And you may even find yourself in physical danger; we'll explore this further in Chapter 11.

Now, toxic relationships aren't unhealthy all the time—and that can be one of the most confusing things about them. When things are good, you wonder why it can't always be that way. And then, the toxic part of the relationship kicks in. This pattern is typical of the cycle of abuse. **If your relationship is good 90 percent of the time, but unhealthy 10 percent of the time, it is still a toxic relationship. Just because someone is good to you sometimes doesn't erase the abusive behavior.**

"When I was with him, nothing could have been better. Except for the time he pushed me down a flight of stairs. And slapped me. And stalked me."

—Pam, 29

Is It Abuse?

Sometimes, when I meet with clients and refer to what they endured as "abuse," there is an initial resistance. You may be hesitant to use the word *abuse* when describing your relationship. You might be thinking, *He had an anger issue, but I wouldn't call it abuse*, or *We just clashed a lot about things*. It's important to recognize that abusive behavior takes many forms. We often think of abuse in terms of physical violence—hitting, kicking, and slapping, for example. Even if the other person never acted physically violent toward you, the relationship may still have been abusive. Abuse may be physical, sexual, financial/economic, verbal, or emotional/psychological. Emotional and psychological abuse, which are also referred to as *coercive control*, can be just as damaging as physical abuse.

The goal of the abuser, in all these types of abuse, is to gain control and power. The more dependent you are on the abuser, and the longer you stay, the less likely it is that you will leave. Abusers know this. Abusers also have a vested interest in making sure you don't talk to other people about the abuse.

Ask yourself whether the other person has ever done any of the following:

Physical Abuse
- Pinching you
- Tickling you excessively
- Blocking your exit or escape
- Biting you or spitting at you
- Hitting, kicking, punching, slapping
- Abandoning you by stranding you somewhere, kicking you out of a vehicle, or refusing to take you back home

Sexual Abuse
- Ridiculing your body or sexual performance
- Making you "earn" sex
- "Punishing" you through refusing sex
- Having sex with you while you are sleeping or unconscious
- Forcing you into sexual acts (rape)

Financial/Economic Abuse
- Putting you on an "allowance"
- Refusing to include or removing your name from any financial documents

- Refusing to buy food or clothing
- Withholding money from you as "punishment"
- Forcing you to turn your income over to him or her
- Forcing you into prostitution
- Forcing you to quit your job
- Threatening to tell your employer that you are unstable
- Refusing to give you access to transportation

Verbal Abuse

- Calling you derogatory names
- Yelling and screaming
- Telling you that your clothes are too provocative
- Criticizing you in front of other people
- Undermining you in front of your children

Emotional/Psychological Abuse

- Isolating you from your family and friends
- Pitting you against other people by telling you they have said un-kind things about you (*triangulating*)
- Guilting and shaming you when you show signs of independence
- Questioning your abilities as a parent
- Threatening to take your children away from you
- Shaming you into not disclosing abuse
- Comparing you to others unfavorably
- Making you question your reality (see "What Is Gaslighting?" on page 12)

You may find yourself fighting back against a toxic person by using some of the strategies they use—including yelling, physical violence, or *stonewalling*. You might become upset with yourself for engaging in these behaviors when you know they're wrong. However, fighting back against a narcissist with abusive behaviors doesn't make you a bad person. You are trying to survive in an impossible situation. You may have been threatened physically or emotionally. You may have been blocked from leaving. Sometimes, just to get through the day, victims of domestic violence, including emotional abuse, resort to the behaviors that the toxic person usually uses—*because sometimes it makes the abuser stop.*

When you use the same behaviors an abusive person has displayed toward you, it is called *reactive abuse.* It doesn't mean you are abusive. The abuser, however, may tell you that you are really the abuser, not her. She may tell you that she is really the victim. Don't believe it. A good thing to look at is your pattern of behavior throughout your life. If you generally did not act out in an abusive manner earlier in life, the chances are that you were reacting to being abused. Now, you may be feeling that the toxic person is being held to a higher standard than you and that you're getting a pass for your own problematic behavior. That is a normal feeling. Behavior in response to a real threat is a form of defense—it doesn't mean you are abusive.

"He told me my job was taking up too much of my time and that he needed me at home. I quit. I realize now that he was just trying to isolate me."

—Ginger, 50

"I told her I didn't like the way she was treating me. She kicked me out of the car in the middle of nowhere and sped off."

—Melissa, 43

Once you exit a relationship with an abusive person, it is important to attend counseling so you can work through any shame and guilt you may have from using the abuser's behaviors against her. For more information on counseling, see Chapter 6.

What Is Gaslighting?

Gaslighting is a form of psychological and emotional abuse. It is a series of manipulation techniques where an abuser makes a victim question his reality. Over time, the victim feels as if he is losing his mind and that he cannot trust his own perception of the world. He then relies more on the gaslighter to determine the "correct" version of reality.

The gaslighter's ultimate goal is to gain control and power over a person in a bid to get all their attention. You see gaslighting behaviors in people with narcissistic or *sociopathic* traits and in people diagnosed with narcissistic personality disorder, among other mental health disorders.

Gaslighting behaviors include the following:

- Telling you that you didn't see or hear something
- Cheating often, but obsessively accusing you of being unfaithful
- Saying that other people think you are crazy
- Sabotaging your work
- Pressuring you through guilt and shame
- Hiding your valuable items, then blaming you
- Telling you that others treated her much better than you have
- Telling you that you are the only person who has had issues with her
- Knowing your psychological weaknesses and exploiting them

Gaslighting is a slow, insidious process and builds up over time. Because the purpose of gaslighting is to make a person question their sanity, if you've experienced it, it's very important that you meet with a mental health professional to discuss it. I strongly recommend individual therapy rather than couples therapy, as a gaslighter may try to manipulate the therapist and will usually blame you for any issues. For more information on mental health professionals, see Chapter 6.

If You're Being Mistreated at Work

When a person's behavior has impacted your ability to do your job or stay at your place of employment, it qualifies as harassment. That person could be your boss, a coworker, or even someone who isn't an employee (such as a client). The inappropriate or harmful behavior doesn't necessarily need to be directed toward you; if you feel unsafe in a work environment that tolerates bullying and other abusive behavior, or you've witnessed someone being bullied, it also qualifies. In the United States, workplace harassment, including sexual harassment, is a form of employment discrimination that violates several federal laws. See "Working with a High-Conflict Person" on page 37 for more.

How Did This Happen to Me?

To figure out how to get out of a toxic relationship or heal from one you have ended, it's often helpful to look into how and why you got into one. There are several factors that make anyone more vulnerable to a toxic person and also make it harder to leave—and you have no control over many of them. These factors include growing up in a dysfunctional family, self-esteem issues, trauma bonding, societal pressure, lack of resources, the sunk cost theory, and experiencing cognitive dissonance.

Family of Origin Issues

We learn how to conduct ourselves in a relationship by watching our families. Think back on your parents' relationship while you were growing up. Did they calmly discuss issues, or did they have big fights? Did you try to become almost invisible so they didn't take out their anger on you? We tend to repeat patterns in our lives. If you grew up in a home where chaos ruled, you might find that it feels normal to you to have big ups and downs in your relationships as an adult. If you are in a healthy relationship or friendship, the sense of calm can seem boring to you. You may also feel that a healthy relationship is too good to be true, and you are just waiting for "the other shoe to drop." You have a sense that something terrible is going to happen because things are going relatively well. You may have to still maintain contact with a toxic family member that caused you to have unhealthy views of relationships. You may have blamed yourself for the toxic person's behavior, as you were told it was your fault.

The dynamics in your family of origin have a big influence on your attachment style as an adult. Your attachment style is the particular way in which you relate to and bond with other people. We'll explore this concept in depth in Chapter 5.

JOURNAL PROMPT: WHERE HAVE I SEEN THESE BEHAVIORS BEFORE?

Is this the first time you have encountered a toxic person? Or have you had encounters with several narcissists or sociopaths in your life? Take time to write down the times in your childhood when you encountered someone who did not have your best interests in mind. It could have been a family member, friend, teacher, coach, or other person who had an impact on your life. Describe their unhealthy behaviors, using the list of toxic behaviors found earlier in this chapter. Add what your relationship is like with them now. Do you still see or talk to them often? Have you distanced yourself from them? Or are they no longer alive?

JOURNAL PROMPT: HOW DID TOXIC PEOPLE CHANGE MY CHILDHOOD?

Using the list of people you created in the previous journal exercise, write how each of those toxic people impacted how you viewed yourself and the world around you. You may have received the message from a critical parent that you weren't good enough; you may have learned from your teacher that boundaries were permeable; you may have learned from a coach that it was acceptable to be yelled at on a regular basis. By creating this list, you are identifying areas to work on in protecting yourself from toxic people. If you are in therapy, consider sharing this activity with your mental health professional.

Self-Esteem Issues

Self-esteem is your subjective sense of your own worth or abilities; low self-esteem can make you vulnerable to a toxic person or situation because it can be harder to set or maintain boundaries. Issues with low self-esteem can arise from growing up in a dysfunctional family, but you may have also experienced one of the following:

- Bullying in school or in the workplace
- Difficulties with academic and/or work performance
- A history of difficulty achieving goals
- A history of anxiety, depression, bipolar disorder, or attention deficit hyperactivity disorder (ADHD)
- Being ostracized or marginalized
- A history of unhealthy relationships
- A history of abuse
- Chronic medical issues
- Chronic stress
- Difficulty getting basic life needs met, such as housing or food

When you have low self-esteem, you may feel responsible for issues that aren't your fault or feel that you "caused" a toxic person to treat you poorly. You may feel that no one else will tolerate you if you cut ties with the toxic person. You may never feel good enough. But you do have a right to be here. You also have the right to be treated with dignity and respect. One of the most powerful feelings is knowing you can walk away from a relationship or situation that is not in your best interest.

CHECK-IN: HOW IS YOUR SELF-WORTH?

Your self-worth is a significant determinant of how easily you can forgive yourself. See if you agree or disagree with the following statements.

1. I generally feel pretty good about my life.
2. I practice good self-care.
3. I reach out to others for support.
4. I see setbacks as temporary.
5. I think there are valuable lessons to be learned in hard times.
6. Life can sometimes be chaotic, but I feel pretty steady.
7. If someone upsets me, it is reasonably easy for me to get back on track.

8. I realize another person's feelings are his or hers to own and I cannot "fix" or change them.
9. I can set good boundaries that help me live my best life.
10. My emotions are temporary, so I don't let them get the best of me.

The more statements you agreed with, the more likely you are to have good self-worth. This means you can weather life's storms and still feel pretty good about yourself.

If you disagree with most statements, that's okay—building self-esteem takes practice, but it's absolutely something you can cultivate. We'll explore how in Chapters 5, 6, 8, and 10.

Trauma Bonding

Another reason why it might be challenging to end or leave a toxic relationship is due to something called *trauma bonding*, which arises from a cycle of abuse and isolation interspersed with perceived kind and generous behavior by the abuser.[1] It is when a survivor of abuse develops an attachment to or sympathy toward her abuser. Trauma bonding can occur in any interaction where a person is abused, including in domestic violence, child abuse, human trafficking, cults, and hostage situations (in fact, trauma bonding is also sometimes referred to as *Stockholm syndrome*, a term you might recognize; it's named after a hostage situation where the hostages developed an attachment to their captors).

The following characteristics of a relationship help create a trauma bond:

- A power differential between the abuser and survivor
- Intermittent abusive and non-abusive treatment during the relationship
- The survivor experiences intense fear and has a strong will to survive

- The abuser tells the survivor about how his childhood made him abusive and makes excuses for his behavior
- The abuser's behavior escalates upon discovering the survivor has plans to leave or has left the relationship

A trauma bond can take a few days or months to develop. It is not completely known why trauma bonding occurs in abusive relationships, but it may be at least partly due to hormones. To see why, let's take a moment for a short biology lesson. Your autonomic nervous system—or the part of your nervous system that controls your involuntary movements—is made up of the *sympathetic* nervous system (SNS) and the *parasympathetic* nervous system (PNS). In simplest terms, SNS gets your body ready to weather stressful events and the PNS returns your body to its normal state afterward. When you have a fight or experience conflict, your SNS activates. Your adrenal glands send the hormone adrenaline into your body, triggering a cascade of other hormones to put your body on high alert—your heart rate and blood pressure increase, your breathing becomes more rapid, and your senses sharpen. This is the "fight, flight, or freeze" response. When you are in an abusive relationship, you are more likely to freeze rather than fight or flee because you are in survival mode. This can result in a feeling of helplessness, depression, low self-esteem, and increased bonding with your abuser.[2] When you make up after conflict, your PNS takes over. Your pituitary gland releases a hormone called oxytocin into your system (this also happens when you have general physical or emotional closeness to a person). Oxytocin helps promote bonding. So, the monster you are with now turns into a not-so-bad person—and the process continues.

When you have been through trauma with your partner (even if your partner was the perpetrator), you tend to lean on her to make sense of what has happened. It might be hard for an outside observer to understand, but your brain seeks to make sense of abuse—and the closest person to it is the person who perpetrated it. This creates a cycle of attachment through trauma.

Signs of trauma bonding include

* Blaming yourself for the abuse
* Blaming others for the person's abusive behavior
* Avoiding any behaviors that might set the abuser off
* Becoming preoccupied with and anticipating the abuser's needs and wants
* Having a detailed accounting of the abuser's schedule and habits

Bonding is a biological process. The stress you feel when you have separated from a toxic person is based on brain chemicals. Look at the process of a toxic relationship as one of addiction and that you are currently experiencing withdrawal symptoms. The withdrawal symptoms will get better with time. This is why it is so important to cut off contact with a toxic person, as much as possible—you need time to heal from the highs and lows. (We'll discuss this more in the next chapter.)

"He told me I was the most amazing person he had ever met. Almost the day after he asked me if I was '100 percent in' the relationship, I started seeing who he really was."

—Jameela, 26

Societal Pressure

As you're thinking about what might have kept you in a toxic situation, reflect on the messaging you may be encountering on social media or from the people around you. Our society wants us to be in and stay in relationships. You may have heard sayings like "love and respect your family, no matter what; they're the only ones you have" or "blood is thicker than water." Society also emphasizes that being in a relationship is better than being single—even if the dynamic is unhealthy.

There's also a toxic positivity that permeates social media and pop psychology. The ideas that you should "always look on the bright side" and "always try harder" put pressure on people who are just trying to get through the day. These pressures can make you question whether it is worth it to cut ties with unhealthy people. Envy and self-blame set in.

Lack of Access to Resources

Money doesn't buy happiness, but it can make life a lot easier. If you have access to housing, counseling services, and transportation, you are more able to leave a toxic relationship. This is exactly why a toxic person may try to limit your ability to earn your own income or restrict you from having access to a vehicle. This form of abuse, known as *economic abuse*, limits your independence and keeps you right where a toxic person wants you—under his control.

"It would have been much easier to leave if he hadn't convinced me that I was 'bad with money' and needed to sign everything over to him."

—Alejandro, 32

Sunk Cost Effect

When you are in a toxic relationship, it can be challenging to leave when you have invested time and effort into making it work. Part of the reason for this is that people tend to experience the *sunk cost effect*. You want to feel that everything you gave up to make the relationship work was worth it, so you put more time into it even if it's not in your best interest.[3] You don't want to feel you "wasted" that time, so you're less likely to leave or end the relationship. However, consider that if you had kept up a relationship with this person, it would have cost you even more time and effort.

Cognitive Dissonance

When you first met the toxic person, she probably didn't appear to be toxic, but when you were in the relationship, you started seeing unhealthy behaviors. Those behaviors didn't fit with what you knew about that person, and they challenged your ideas of people being good. When you have been taught to avoid relationships with unhealthy people yet find yourself with someone who treats you poorly, it can be a very confusing experience. This person treats you the opposite of how you were taught people should treat you. So, why is it so difficult to leave and rebuild?

When someone you care about treats you in a way that doesn't make sense, your brain feels kind of scrambled. This is called *cognitive dissonance*. Cognitive dissonance happens when you receive information that contradicts your beliefs and doesn't make sense with what you know about people and the world around you. When we receive information that is the opposite of what we know to be accurate, we do one of the following:

> "First I told myself that I had already been working there for three months, so why not ride it out and see if things get better. Then it was six months later . . . then a year later. I worried I wouldn't be able to find another job. Then I was concerned that I would have a big gap on my résumé since I had now been working there for two years. Eventually I realized that I had spent a lot of time trying to adapt to a dysfunctional environment."
>
> —Donna, 52

- Ignore new information
- Commit even further to our beliefs
- Avoid exposure to contradictory information
- Project our feelings of being overwhelmed onto others
- Absorb the contradictory information and change our existing beliefs
- Accept the conflicting information as it is and accept holding two different beliefs

Cognitive dissonance is the feeling that something is not sitting right with you and contradicts your existing belief system. You can try to stuff those unpleasant feelings down, but they keep popping up. You may use drugs and alcohol to numb the feeling of competing beliefs. You feel stuck in a toxic situation.

To stop cognitive dissonance and rebuild your life, you first need to learn more about it. Consider seeing a mental health professional to help you untangle the messages you received during the relationship from your current beliefs. (Again, we'll cover working with mental health professionals in depth in Chapter 6.)

JOURNAL PROMPT: WHICH FACTORS HAVE INFLUENCED YOU?

Of the factors you read about, which influenced your ability to leave a toxic relationship or situation?

- Family of origin issues
- Self-esteem issues
- Trauma bonding
- Societal pressure
- Lack of access to resources
- Sunk cost effect
- Cognitive dissonance

Which of these factors caused the most issues for you? What can you do in the future to become aware if one or more of these factors are influencing your relationships?

• • • • •

By now, you've learned how to identify the signs of an unhealthy relationship. You learned that abuse isn't just physical—it can also take the form of emotional, verbal, sexual, and financial/economic abuse. You learned about why you might have been drawn into a toxic situation, including family of origin issues, trauma bonding, cognitive dissonance, and other factors. In the next chapter, we'll turn to an essential first step in the healing process: blocking contact, if possible.

2

BLOCK CONTACT IF YOU CAN

How to Prevent Unwanted Contact from a Toxic
Person, and What to Do When You Can't

AYA HAD TRIED TO LEAVE HER HUSBAND, LOU, BEFORE—ENOUGH TIMES that she could almost predict how it would play out. When she had tried to leave when he was home, he would grab her, block doorways, or stand in front of her car, refusing to move until she capitulated. When she had managed to leave the house, Lou would lie low for a few days and then start blowing up her phone with calls and text messages, promising her things would change if she'd come back. She knew her only way to escape was when he wasn't home—and this time, she decided, she wouldn't engage when he inevitably called or texted.

Aya felt guilty for leaving like this, but she felt her husband had given her no choice. At first, she didn't block his phone number or email because she was worried about him. His first texts asked, pleaded, to let him know she was okay. When she didn't answer, the texts became angrier and angrier, calling her a bitch and a traitor. When that failed to get a response, he switched tactics again: "I love you. I miss you. You're the most incredible woman I've ever met." The one thing her husband never said in his texts was that he was sorry. Although she missed him, that gave her the resolve she needed to make a clean break this time.

Aya felt proud that she was standing her ground and refusing to engage, but every time her phone buzzed or beeped, she got a rush of adrenaline. After a few weeks, she realized the physical toll it was taking on her: she felt jittery and on edge pretty much all the time, and she was having trouble sleeping at night. She then blocked his number and his email address, figuring she'd covered any way he could contact her. That night, she finally got some much needed rest.

Days later, her phone buzzed with a new text—from Lou's best friend, Enzo, asking whether she was all right. She figured it was okay to reply; she didn't want to worry anyone. "Yes, I'm fine," she texted back.

His response came almost immediately. "Lou is really upset and wants you to come home," the message read.

As she stared at the phone in disbelief, Aya thought, *Seriously, Enzo, you too? How else is he going to find ways to get to me?*

• • • • •

You've finally realized that it's time to move on from a toxic relationship— maybe you left a partner, are deciding to end a friendship, or are distancing yourself from toxic family members. Blocking all contact may be very difficult for you to do. You may be asking yourself why it is so difficult to imagine life without that person, even though you have been treated badly. It is completely understandable that it can be a heart-wrenching choice to cut off contact with someone that was once important in your life.

Even so, this is a crucial step toward healing. So, if you have the option of blocking all contact with a toxic person, do it. In this chapter, we'll cover why blocking contact is so important and how to do it effectively. If you truly can't block contact with the person for any reason, such as if you're related to each other or coparenting, we'll also cover how to manage that situation later in this chapter.

Why It's So Important to Block Contact

A toxic person tends not to change her behavior, even when she gets in trouble for it. She will up the ante by getting more outrageous with her behavior and demands. A toxic person will try to test your boundaries by continuing to contact you after she discarded you or you ended the relationship. She may fly into a *narcissistic rage* and then contact you the next day as if nothing had happened. It may not be a text or phone call; she might use other methods, such as an ex suddenly returning your belongings through the mail.

Some toxic people will wait months or even years before contacting you again. Silence is not a sign that the person has moved on, and it shouldn't be taken as such. Toxic people "recycle" exes and friends and will contact you when they need an attention fix.

Maybe this isn't the first time you've tried to end this relationship. As you learned in Chapter 1, toxic people often try to hoover you back into a relationship. Whatever they promise you usually turns out to not be true, and the relationship becomes just as problematic as it was before. Leaving the lines of communication open with this person leaves you at risk. When you reply to a toxic person hoovering you, especially after her outrageous behavior toward you, it sends a message to her that you will accept that level of abuse from her.

As you read in Chapter 1, a relationship with a toxic person can be like a potent drug: this type of relationship is full of highs and lows. You may have developed a trauma bond with the toxic person, where you had periods of abuse followed by calm. You may even be experiencing feelings of withdrawal now that you have limited contact with the toxic person. You may feel a deep sense of loss, to the point where you have a physical ache. You may experience insomnia or brain fog. Your limbs may feel heavy, and you may feel like you are moving slower than usual. You may also experience shaking and obsessive thoughts. You may think that just contacting the toxic person will make you feel better. But all it does is start the withdrawal cycle over again. To recover from an addiction, you need to cut off the addictive substance, or person.

Steps to Block Contact

Some of this may seem obvious, but in our very connected world, there may be some avenues to contact you that you haven't thought of before. So, use the following checklist to make sure you have everything covered. Block the following:

- Cell/mobile numbers
- Work numbers
- Personal email
- Work email
- All social media accounts: Facebook, Instagram, Snapchat, TikTok, LinkedIn, etc.
- Accounts and phone numbers of her family
- If needed, accounts and phone numbers of mutual friends (see the next section)

Then, change your passwords on

- All streaming services
- Your electronic devices—computer, cell phone, tablet, etc.
- Email accounts
- Data service accounts (cell phone, internet)
- Social media accounts
- Banking and financial accounts
- Work and school accounts

In addition, remove the person from any geolocating apps. You may even need to delete your own social media accounts if you find yourself getting sucked into checking the toxic person's accounts or the accounts of mutual friends. Sometimes, people have found that getting a new phone number, as time- and energy-consuming as it is, is the only way they have been able to get some peace.

If you'll be connected to the person for a limited time, such as while you work through a divorce or other legal proceedings, your attorney can serve as an intermediary. It's understood that you can't totally block some people, such as coparents, but you can go low contact; we'll get to that later in this chapter.

JOURNAL PROMPT: THINKING ABOUT CUTTING OFF CONTACT

Whether to block or limit contact with a toxic person can be a very difficult decision. Think of the toxic person with whom you wish to get some emotional and physical distance. Write down the behaviors she has had that lead you to believe that blocking or limiting contact is the best option. Also write down the times that you have attempted to get away from this person and how it went for you. When you didn't have contact with her, did you have a feeling of relief? Did you have less stress in your life? If the toxic person still attempted to contact you even after you set boundaries about communication, write down the details of what happened. Now write down what you might gain from distancing yourself from this person, and also list the drawbacks. Do the positives outweigh the negatives?

No Flying Monkeys

Blocking a toxic person's family members and your mutual friends may sound extreme. However, a toxic person will often use family members, mutual friends, or coworkers to get messages to you—even if you've cut off contact with him, like Lou's friend Enzo in Aya's story at the beginning of the chapter. These message carriers are called *flying monkeys.*

Being told that a toxic person wants you back in his life, even if it is a message from a secondary source, can pull you back into a toxic dynamic. Sometimes, flying monkeys don't know the truth about what you went through with this person. Remember, some toxic people make it a point to look good to others while hiding their behavior in a relationship.

If you can, block flying monkeys as well. That's what Aya had to do—after Enzo reached out, she blocked him. Other mutual friends were posting a lot of pictures with Lou on social media, causing Aya a lot of distress—so she eventually decided to block them as well. If you see an unknown or unrecognized number on your caller ID, do not answer.

Let your friends and family know that you will not be entertaining any messages sent from the toxic person through them. If a friend or family member tries to talk to you about him, set a boundary and say, "That is off-limits" or "That's a no-fly zone." Walk away if he or she continues to share information about the toxic person.

Now, many times, people who are "recruited" to carry messages from the toxic person don't have bad intent and don't realize they're doing harm. When you set the boundary, anyone who is truly caring of you will acknowledge it and apologize for crossing the line. Boundaries are nonnegotiable. You may have to act on a boundary that you have set if it has been violated. If a flying monkey continues to send you messages from a toxic person, or offers you unsolicited advice after you've asked them not to, it's time to distance yourself or cut off contact with that person. (We'll cover setting and maintaining boundaries in Chapter 5.)

"My aunt was acting as a 'messenger' for my mother. She would start a conversation about something unrelated to my mom and then would sneak in, 'You know, your mother is really trying to work with you here' and similar comments. I finally told her that talking about my mom was off-limits, and if she insisted on bringing my mom up, I would need to limit my contact with her. She hasn't brought up my mother since."

—Amara, 48

Recognize Emotional Blackmail

You may have family members or friends that threaten to hurt or kill themselves when you tell them you need to limit contact. A toxic partner might have threatened self-harm when you told him you were leaving. You may have even had a person threaten to hurt herself when you tell her that you aren't okay with her behavior. Threats like this are known as *emotional blackmail.* Its purpose is to keep you in contact with the person by making you feel guilty.

A person that does this to you is very unhealthy and may have used emotional blackmail in other ways in the past. For instance, he could refuse to go on a planned trip or family gathering that is important to you, or threaten to disinvite you from an event that he knew you were excited about. He may tell you that you treat your ex, family members, or friends better than you treat him. These are all ways that a person induces fear, guilt, or shame in you so he can remain in control.

Recognize that this is merely a control tactic; I know it is difficult to hear, but don't give in. We'll cover dealing with feelings of guilt in Chapter 4. If you are with someone who threatens self-harm or threatens to harm you, contact 911.

> "My boyfriend would threaten to kill himself when I'd tell him I wanted out of the relationship. After I broke up with him, I reconnected with my mother. And guess what she said when I told her I needed to distance myself from her for my mental health. Yep, same thing."
>
> —Bryce, 45

Protect Yourself from Harassment

If you stop contact with a toxic person, she may start following you or contacting you repeatedly. She may show up at your home unannounced. The best option tends to be not giving the toxic person any attention and hoping that she moves on. She may get a new number for the purposes of harassing you, so don't answer unknown calls. Don't post on social media in real time. If you post photos of a place you visited, do it after you have changed locations. You may not want to even post locations on social media, as the person harassing you may start frequenting those locations to see if they can spot you. Let your neighbors and property management know that this person is bothering you, and to please let you know if they see her around your home. If you receive any threats, contact law enforcement. In cases where your well-being is threatened, you may qualify for a court-issued restraining order. While a restraining order doesn't prevent someone from coming to your work or home, you do have legal support in case that does happen.

What to Do When You Can't Cut Contact

There may be times when you cannot completely cut off contact with someone, such as if you have children together or still work at the same company. You may have a family member that you can't completely block, especially if you plan on spending time with other family members during holidays and other celebrations. You may be in a work climate where getting another job is a remote possibility. You still need to protect your own interests even when you can't completely cut off contact with a toxic person or situation. In the following pages, we'll look at how to do it.

Coparenting with a High-Conflict Person

If you are coparenting with a high-conflict toxic person, establishing healthy boundaries is key. In Chapter 5, "Establish Boundaries," we'll cover this topic in more detail. For now, I'd like to hit on some important early steps so that you can minimize contact with a toxic coparent.

Find a Good Family Law Attorney

Now is the time to become an advocate for yourself and your children. Meet with different attorneys to find one that is the best fit for you. Get referrals from trusted friends and family members or people you know that have experienced coparenting with a toxic person. Ask the attorney whether she has experience working with people who are coparenting with narcissists and other high-conflict people.

Let your attorney know your experience with the toxic person. Although discussing your issues with your coparent is a very emotional topic, write down specific details and incidences, not just how you feel. While it is okay to make such speculations as "I think he might get enraged if we want to change time-sharing," say why that is the case. If your coparent has a high-conflict personality or has threatened you physically or financially, let your attorney know.

You may also need the services of a parent coordinator who can work with you and your coparent instead of leaving the two of you to fight issues out over the phone. A parent coordinator is a neutral third party, usually a mental health professional, who helps parents create and stick to a parenting plan. She can also help coparents work through schedule changes, major decisions (e.g., a change in schooling), or any decision where there is a disagreement. A parent coordinator has received specialized training in working with high-conflict coparents. You can hire one on your own or use one who is appointed by the court. Usually you and the coparent will first meet individually with the parent coordinator and then meet together, not only to discuss concerns and document changes, but also so that each parent has accountability for their actions. (See Resources for help in locating an attorney and pro bono resources.)

"I found an attorney that I really 'clicked' with. He had a good understanding of what I was dealing with, and clearly explained possible options with me."

—Anoush, 36

Create a Solid Parenting Plan

You may need a detailed parenting plan where every coparenting issue is addressed—meaning, you have set rules around the following:

- Where and when will exchanges take place, and who will be present? (In high-conflict coparenting situations, parents may consider choosing a neutral location and having family members exchange the children.)
- For how long do you need to wait with your children at an exchange location before time-sharing reverts to you (if the coparent has not notified you of being late)?
- Who will have the children on each holiday, and when will pickup and drop-off occur on those holidays?
- Who has final decision-making power (or will it be a joint decision) regarding school, medical issues and providers, after-school activities, and more?
- Who will pay what for school-related costs, after-school activities, medical visits? How will those expenses be submitted for reimbursement?
- To whom do you give approval to watch your children, and whom do you not want around the children for any reason?

- How far ahead of time do the coparents need to notify if they want to take a trip out of state with the child? How about out of the country? (Parents have added that any trips outside the country must be approved by them, and the countries must be part of the Hague Convention, which helps return children to their custodial parents if they are abducted by the noncustodial parent and taken out of their home country.)
- Do you require an itinerary for any trips taken out of the local area? How many days or weeks before the trip do you wish to receive the itinerary?
- What schools will the children be attending in the future? You can also add that when your child is in a certain grade, the coparents will revisit the school issue.
- Who will claim the children as dependents on their tax return? (Some parents alternate years if the time-sharing is 50-50.)
- How will the coparents communicate with each other? Will communication be conducted solely via a coparenting app so as to decrease conflict?

In addition to these questions, which you should answer according to what makes sense for your unique situation, I recommend establishing the following hard rules:

- The coparent will have uninterrupted access to speak with the child during designated call times.
- Neither parent will make disparaging remarks about the other parent in front of the child, or when the child is present in the home. Neither parent will leave custody or divorce documents out in view of the child. Neither parent will discuss coparenting finances in front of the child.
- You have a right to first refusal. If your coparent will be absent from the home for a certain amount of time during their time-share, they must first contact you to see whether you would like to have

the children instead of your coparent contacting a sitter or family member.

Having strict parameters on your parenting plan can be a pain for you because it limits your own flexibility, but they also help keep a toxic coparent in line. If you and the coparent have a disagreement about a child-related issue, you can always go to the parenting plan as the final answer. You can create a parenting plan with your attorney or with a parent coordinator.

Meet on Neutral Territory (or Not at All)

When it's time to switch off, instead of going to each other's houses, consider exchanging your child at a neutral location, such as at a public place. Or have another trusted family member exchange your child with the coparent. Parenting plans can state how long you need to wait for the coparent to show up without hearing from them before the time-sharing reverts to you.

"We used to do pickup and drop-off at our houses, but that usually caused some kind of issue. I didn't want my son seeing that. So now we do pickup and drop-off only at school. We rarely have to see each other anymore."

—Eiko, 32

Use a Dedicated App to Communicate

You may also want to consider limiting your contact with the coparent to a parenting app rather than allowing your ex to call or text you. For more information on parenting apps, see the Resources section at the end of this book. You can add to your parenting plan that communication will only be with the app. Coparenting apps time-stamp when the coparent receives and reads a message, so it stops them from trying to make the excuse that they didn't see it.

Besides helping you maintain a boundary, some apps have additional features you may like. For instance, some apps have a setting that notifies you if you are using wording in your message that might be inappropriate or inflammatory. Some apps also make it possible to submit receipts to the coparent for reimbursement.

Consider Parallel Parenting

In standard coparenting, the parents are civil to each other and have reasonable expectations that they can work out issues together. Coparents may have similar guidelines and rules in each home so that children feel more of a sense of stability. Parents both attend their children's events and doctor's appointments, with minimal disagreement. However, if you are coparenting with a toxic person, having respectful discussions and seeing each other at your children's events may not be possible. This can be especially true if the relationship involved domestic violence. Being present at the same event may present an opportunity for the toxic coparent to gain control or intimidate you.

In these situations, parallel parenting might be an option. Parallel parenting is a style of coparenting where you keep everything separate. You don't attend anything with your coparent, including after-school events or doctor's appointments. You only communicate with the coparent in writing, such as only speaking to each other via a coparenting app. You only communicate with the coparent when it's absolutely necessary. Instead of the coparent reporting to you what happened at a doctor's appointment, you can contact the doctor for that information.

In a parallel parenting model, sometimes one parent is named as a "primary parent" in a parenting plan. This means that one parent has final decision-making authority for the child. A primary parent is established so parents need to communicate less with each other. Be prepared to have a copy of the parenting agreement for any physicians or therapists helping your child. They may want a document signed by a judge that states who has medical decision-making rights.

Parallel coparenting can help you in a variety of ways. It limits contact. You may find that you experience less conflict with the coparent when your lives are kept almost completely separate. You also may have more time to focus on your child's well-being instead of fending off verbal attacks and emotional abuse from the coparent. Your children will benefit as well—children of divorced parents have fewer behavior issues when there is less coparenting conflict.[1] By having a detailed parenting plan, boundaries are already established. You can always refer to the parenting plan if your coparent is trying to violate boundaries. Most important, the quality of your relationship with your child is of the utmost importance in determining their quality of life and relationships in the future.[2]

Standard Coparenting

- Both parents consult with each other about decisions and work together for the child's well-being.
- Both parents attend child's events, holidays, and birthdays.
- Coparents communicate via phone, text, or email.
- Disagreements may occur, but eventually the coparents come to an agreement.
- Exchange of the child is done at either parent's home.
- Changes in parents' schedules are usually accommodated by other parent if enough notice is given.
- Coparents work together to have similar guidelines and structure in each home.

Parallel Coparenting

- Communication is only done via a coparenting app, such as Our Family Wizard or Talking Parents.
- Coparents alternate attending child's games or other activities, or one parent doesn't attend those activities.
- Holidays and birthdays are spent separately with the child.
- Each parent follows their own schedule and logistics and sets their own rules.
- One parent has decision-making authority on child's medical care, schooling, and after-school activities, or coparents have decision-making authority in different domains.

"My kid's father took any opportunity to harass me, including cornering me at our kid's soccer and baseball games. I spoke to my attorney about it, and it is now written in the parenting plan that we alternate attending games."

—Remi, 40

- Child's schedule is maintained in a shared online calendar or in a coparenting app, with no other communication between the parents.
- Exchange of the child is done in a public place, with no contact between the coparents or by other family members.
- Changes in the parents' schedules are handled over a coparenting app, and it is not assumed that the other parent will accommodate the change.

Managing Limited Contact with a Family Member

You may not be able to fully cut off contact with a relative because the members of your family that you get along with still include the toxic person at family gatherings or holidays. You might even work with a toxic family member. If you can't go no contact, try limiting your contact as much as possible. Although you can excuse yourself from attending family gatherings, you may not choose that option because it means missing out on seeing the rest of your family.

If you do attend a family gathering, limit the amount of time you spend there. If you have a trusted family member, have them keep a lookout for potential conflict while you are there. If the toxic person appears to be headed toward you, a family member can distract and divert them. You could also hold separate gatherings for your family where you don't invite the toxic person, but you can be sure that someone in the family will let her know.

Although it would be nice to think that you could just tell your toxic family member that they are upsetting you, that can be all the fuel a toxic person needs. They get energy from someone being bothered by them. It's better to avoid the person than interact with them. If you can't avoid interacting with them, try to emotionally detach as much as possible. It can be helpful to picture yourself as an outside observer to the situation. For example, view yourself as a sociologist collecting data. Or, use the "gray rock" technique, where you respond to a toxic person in the least responsive way possible. Give short or one-word answers to questions.

Keep your voice tone calm and even. Appear as boring as possible. When a toxic person realizes that their "bait" isn't working, sometimes they decrease the harassing behavior. Also consider meeting with a mental health professional (which we'll cover in Chapter 6) to discover healthy ways to detach.

If you have a toxic parent who is aging, you may be asked to take care of her. You may be an only child, so the burden is placed directly on you. You are under no obligation to take care of an abusive parent. Although friends and family may tell you that you "owe it" to your parent, they don't know what damage and stress she caused you. Your friends and family may also be trying to get out of taking care of your parent themselves.

> "I do the 'gray rock' method with my sister since I am unable to completely cut off contact. I stick to facts and don't show any emotion. It can be really hard to do, but it is getting easier each time."
>
> —Joan, 65

Working with a High-Conflict Person

Shira had been working for the same company for six years. She got along well with her old boss, Cindy, but she had resigned several months ago. The new boss, Devon, seemed to be targeting Shira, and she didn't know why. He would routinely call on her during meetings and ask her questions that he knew she wouldn't be able to answer. She would bring home-cooked meals to work, and Devon would loudly ask who brought the "weird food," knowing it was Shira's lunch. He would tell Shira that an assignment was due at the end of the week, but on Wednesday or Thursday, he would yell at her about not getting the assignment done on time. Shira felt her boss was working at embarrassing her in front of their coworkers.

Shira approached Devon and told him that she felt she was being treated unfairly. This was all the ammunition Devon needed. When he put Shira on the spot at meetings, he made a point of asking her if she felt she was "being treated unfairly" by being asked questions. Devon called a meeting with Shira and two of her coworkers. When Shira showed up at

Devon's office, he told her that the coworkers couldn't attend the meeting. Shira got a sick feeling in the pit of her stomach. This didn't feel right to her at all. She told Devon that she would not be able to meet with him and quickly exited his office.

If you, like Shira, are stuck working with a toxic individual, here are some steps that you can take to keep your contact as minimal as possible.

Know the Rules and Explore Your Options

In many cases, reporting the behavior to your human resources (HR) department is the way to go. Before you do, review your employer's guidelines for reporting bullying and harassment. Then, if you have the resources, consult with an attorney who specializes in workplace issues and can help you explore your options. I especially recommend getting professional advice if the company you work for doesn't have reporting guidelines; also, some workplaces don't have to follow the Equal Employment Opportunity Commission (EEOC) harassment guidelines. If you do decide to report, your HR professional may be able to help you navigate dealing with the person and provide backup to protect you. But do know that HR can do only so much—and if you're experiencing conflict with a manager or someone in power at your company, you may be dissatisfied with the resolution they can offer you.

Ask for Space

If you can, approach your manager to see if they can help get some distance between you and the high-conflict coworker. Ask if it's possible to be reassigned from projects you may be working on together. If your work areas are close by, ask if you might be moved. If your workplace is large enough, you may be able to transfer to another department or floor. If you work the same shift, consider changing yours. You are still able to work for the same company, but you are limiting your interactions with the toxic person.

Avoid Being Alone with the Person

If you work with a toxic person, she may try to isolate you. You may be told that you have to meet alone with her. Bring a trusted coworker to the meeting or decline to meet with her. Avoid being the only other person at the office besides the toxic person. If there is no one else there, you have no witnesses.

"My boss routinely told me I needed to work late on certain days. Not coincidentally, he would be the only other person in the office. He has had a history of being inappropriate. I said a firm 'no' the next time he told me I needed to stay late. I have consulted an attorney and the human resources department at my office."

—Jesse, 28

Write It Down

Keep written documentation of issues, including date, time, and direct quotes. Keep it factual. Don't use an employer-owned device to keep documentation. Your employer has full access to your devices on their network. If you are fired or leave your job, you might need to turn over the device immediately.

Minimize Them on Teleconferencing

If you are working from home and have to attend teleconferencing with this person, seeing her face can cause you anxiety. Minimize the screen or put a smiley face on a sticky note and put it on the screen over her face. It may sound silly, but being able to avoid looking at a person that has caused you pain can be a relief.

Ask for a Work-Home Hybrid

If you work on location and are around a toxic coworker, ask your employer whether you can work from home or do a work-home hybrid, where you spend three days at home and two days at the office. You can ask for this type of work model without saying that you want to get away from someone at the office. You may need to emphasize that your productivity will be the same or you may be even more productive if you work from home. Employers have become more comfortable with this style of work. If you are able to transition to only working from home, you may need to go into the office just for specific project meetings.

Look for Another Job

Even though it seems unfair that you would have to find another job when someone else is being toxic, sometimes that's what it takes for you to take care of yourself. Your coworker or boss may have behavior that falls short of harassment or bullying, and your employer won't take steps to remedy the situation. It may be time for you to seek other employment. You may find that working in a healthier environment results in you feeling better, both emotionally and physically. Workplace abuse has been associated with depression, anxiety, difficulties sleeping, injuries, and poorer quality of life.[3]

• • • • •

Blocking all forms of contact, if possible, is the best way to remove a toxic person from your life. But if you can't entirely cut the toxic person out of your life, you still have things you can do—setting rules with a toxic coparent, limiting contact and detaching from a family member, and getting space and consulting with an attorney about harassment at work. All these measures are important steps to protect yourself from further abuse and manipulation—an essential step on your road to healing. The next step? We'll explore what you can do if you aren't getting closure after leaving a toxic situation.

3

(FOR)GET CLOSURE

Why It's Hard to Find Resolution After a Toxic
Relationship, and How to Move On Without It

A FTER TWENTY-FIVE YEARS OF MARRIAGE AND TWO CHILDREN, TAMMY
had finally had enough. For years, Tammy's family and friends told
her that her marriage wasn't abusive because there was no physical violence. However, when she started therapy, her therapist said that there
were different forms of abuse—and from what Tammy had told her about
Isaac's name-calling, refusal to take responsibility for his behavior and
blaming Tammy for "making him" yell at her, and telling their children
that they didn't need to listen to her, it sounded like Tammy was experiencing a form of domestic violence.

Two years after she started therapy, and while the kids were away at
college, Tammy hired a moving company for a weekend when Isaac was
on a business trip. She took items and pieces of furniture that were hers
long before the marriage, items that her family had given them, and items
that she solely used in the home. She blocked Isaac's phone numbers and
email addresses, taking the steps outlined in Chapter 2: she limited her
contact with her husband and communicated only through their attorneys. She also let her kids know that Isaac should not be sending messages to her through them. However, because she and Isaac co-owned a

business, Tammy would still have daily contact with him. So, she made a difficult decision: as part of the divorce proceedings, Tammy would sell her part of the business to Isaac. After consulting with her attorney and expressing to him that she was concerned for her safety, Tammy would no longer go on-site at their shared business until the sale was complete.

Tammy wanted the closure that would come with divorce. She wanted Isaac to validate her experiences and apologize for his outrageous behavior. She would settle for his even taking partial responsibility. She wanted him to admit that he had been seeing other women. She believed that when the legal proceedings were wrapped up, she'd finally be able to move on. However, it appeared that Isaac and his attorney were stalling. While negotiations were still underway, Tammy resumed contact with Isaac. She suspected he was just making up reasons to contact her—usually it involved their business, and it always seemed like an "emergency." Tammy felt as if she was in limbo—she wasn't able to get her divorce finalized, and communicating with Isaac was hindering her healing. She felt that she was not going to get the closure she needed to heal until the divorce came through.

Sometimes, You Don't Get Closure

Closure, or getting some sense of completion to your relationship or other loss, is often touted as a "must-have" to heal. However, some losses are so significant that you just don't get that resolution. A pain so deep and devastating may never have a sense of finality to it. And in toxic relationships or situations, you may not get closure as we usually think of it—getting an apology or an admission of wrongdoing from someone who wronged you. You seek validation that what happened to you really happened. You may be seeking some sense of justice or restitution—a toxic person may have stolen money or time from you.

It can be difficult to accept, but a toxic person who never apologized while she was in the relationship is certainly not going to apologize afterward. The exception is if she is trying to hoover you back into having contact with her. But even then apologies are scarce. Why? Well, toxic people don't apologize because they tend to have an *ego-syntonic* personality. This means that they think they are fine and everyone else has a problem. Healthy people tend to have an *ego-dystonic* personality. They realize when something isn't working well for them regarding their behavior, and they may seek help to correct it. It is doubtful that people with an ego-syntonic personality will go to therapy or pursue any other kind of help. They don't think they have a problem. The chances that they will "see the light" and admit their wrongs are minimal to none. If you have had to distance yourself from family members due to their toxic behavior, don't expect them to realize that their behavior and how they treated you was unacceptable. Very rarely will a toxic person take responsibility for his actions. And even if he did admit fault, it would still not be good enough to heal the amount of hurt he caused you.

If something bad happens to a toxic family member, you would think that it would make her realize the error of her ways. You might have heard a story or seen a movie in which an abusive member gets sick, comes close to dying, and realizes she has hurt people—even asks others for forgiveness. Unfortunately, that is rare. If you want closure with this person, you will need to get it from yourself. One way to work on that is through therapy. See Chapter 6, "Talk to a Professional," for more information.

If you work in a toxic environment, unless your experiences meet the legal definition of harassment (and even that doesn't guarantee you'll get justice), you may need to quit your job to have a sense of peace. It's not fair that you have to leave your workplace, but the emotional and physical toll that staying in a toxic workplace is taking on you is not worth it. Your sense of closure may not arrive because you had to make the difficult decision to leave, and you may feel that justice was not served. You thought leaving your toxic job would give you a sense of relief. Instead, you feel sadness and a sense of loss.

Expectations of others' behaviors are tricky things. When we expect people to behave a certain way, we often get disappointed. The only thing we have control over is how we feel and how we interact with others. If you expect a toxic person to apologize or feel any type of remorse for their actions, you may be spending too much time hoping for something that may not happen. Expecting to get closure from another person and then not receiving it can lead to disappointment, frustration, and anger. Not getting closure can lead to having extended feelings of grief (which we will cover in-depth in Chapter 9).

What makes us want those answers to the point where it causes us distress and sleepless nights? Our brain likes to be able to make sense of things. But when it comes to toxic relationships and situations, sometimes they just don't make sense, no matter how many times you try to pick them apart.

There may always be a part of you that wants answers as to how your ex turned out the way she did, how a job that started well ended up such a nightmare, or why your family member seems to be hell-bent on ruining your life. But even if a toxic person told you why she behaved the way she did, it most likely still would not be a good enough answer. Part of the reason that closure is so challenging to achieve after a toxic relationship is that some of what you experienced wasn't real. In the beginning, your ex-partner, friend, or family member most likely created a version of herself that was more appealing and appeared to be less pathological. She might have done this to draw you into her life. Then, the relationship suddenly changed, particularly when you said no to something and set boundaries.

"When I texted my ex to tell him that I needed him to apologize for what he did, he texted back that I was the one that left and that I should be apologizing to him! I gave up on him taking any responsibility."

—Janine, 44

Sometimes, People Don't *Want* You to Get Closure

A toxic ex-partner has a vested interest in not giving you closure. He wants to remain on your mind, so when he decides his new *narcissistic supply* isn't meeting his needs, he can come back to you and hoover you back in. Seeking an answer as to why he did something results in you having contact with him again—and, as we saw in the last chapter, that is precisely what you don't need. The more time you spend around a toxic person, the more likely you will get back into that unhealthy dynamic.

You may even have friends who feed off drama. They may actively try to keep you "stuck" in your trauma or unhealthy situation by encouraging you to return to it. These "friends" are not looking out for your best interests. They are trying to keep you down to either fulfill a need to "rescue" you or to gain some power over you. If you continue to stay in an unhealthy relationship, these friends feed off your stress and enjoy you becoming more dependent on them for reassurance.

Healthy friends encourage you to be the best version of yourself. They lift you up, not actively work at keeping you in an unhealthy mindset or situation. Part of getting closure to a toxic relationship or situation is to also look at whether the people around you are healthy. Even though you may be clinging to any answers or explanations you get from your friends, keep in mind that this "help" may be hurting you. It may be time to cut off contact with these toxic friends, even if it feels as if you are losing your support system. Their support isn't really support—it's harmful.

"My 'friends' were telling me that my job wasn't so bad, that I should just put up with my boss, because other people don't even have jobs. I realized that my friends were just as toxic as my work environment."

—Jake, 28

Closure Is Overrated

Given our deep desire to make sense of our own lives, and our belief in justice, it's only natural that we crave closure, and that it can make our grief more hurtful if we don't get it. But I'm going to say something counterintuitive: closure is overrated. It's okay just to let a loss "be" and not push for resolution. We may still have questions about why things happened the way they did, but over time, those questions will seem to appear in a smaller font in the back of our mind instead of screaming out in capital letters.

To avoid prolonging your pain waiting for closure, take a step back and reflect. You don't necessarily need the finality of a formal apology or resolution to move on with your life and accept that someone treated you poorly. Over time, the loss may resolve itself. You also don't need to get closure to build a happy, healthy life free from toxic people and situations. But if getting a sense of closure is important to your healing process, there are steps you can take to achieve that resolution on your own.

JOURNAL PROMPT: DEFINING CLOSURE

What does closure mean to you? Do you need the person that wronged you to make amends? Do you need a sense of validation or justice? Toxic people have proven time and again that they won't admit fault or make amends. How would you have liked the toxic person to give you closure? What would it feel like if your experience was validated? What other ways can your experience be validated other than from the toxic person?

Moving on Without Closure

What makes us feel satisfied so we are no longer driven to seek answers? Self-introspection; building new memories; spending time with healthy people; and much more. Above all of these, you can find peace by arriving at your own sense of resolution. It may not be the kind of closure you wanted, but it will be enough.

As one example, let's go back to Tammy's story. Although Tammy wanted her husband to apologize for years of emotional and verbal abuse, she knew that would never happen. In therapy, she discovered there were steps she could take to achieve her own resolutions and start healing now. So, instead of waiting for him to say "I'm sorry," with her therapist's guidance, she wrote the apology letter that she wished her husband had given her. Taking steps to achieve her own sense of peace and resolution at least helped Tammy feel that she was making progress in rebuilding her life.

Write an Unsent Letter

We all have things we would like to say to someone, but we can't for various reasons—including that the person has died, or it is not healthy for you to contact him or her. In "unsent letter" journaling, you write down what you would like to tell the person. It can say absolutely whatever you want since you aren't sending it anyway. For instance, you can tell someone how much you appreciate them, how angry they made you, or how you want or don't want to forgive them. You can also use unsent letter journaling as Tammy did—writing down what she wished her husband would have said to her.

Writing a letter to someone, even if you don't send it, can be a cathartic experience. When you write an unsent letter, it helps you get your thoughts—sometimes obsessive thoughts—out of your brain. It helps you free up some "brain space" that was filled with thoughts of the toxic person, giving you at least a temporary decrease in feelings of anxiety, depression, shame, guilt, and grief. Writing your experiences and feelings down also helps you get validation that you otherwise wouldn't receive from the toxic person. As you are writing, be careful not to criticize yourself or judge what you are writing—whatever you write is okay, and it is the truth. There is no judgment, no one telling you that what you experienced didn't happen. Whatever you write is automatically accepted as what happened.

You may find that as you are writing a weight is lifted off you. You may gain a sense of clarity or an "aha!" moment while you are writing an unsent letter. Something that you had been puzzling over in your toxic relationship or in your thoughts about it may suddenly make sense. Other times, reviewing what you have written brings a sense of understanding. For this reason, your letter is also something to consider sharing with your therapist.

Once you have written a few unsent letters, you might realize that you need to do it less and less in order to feel better. When you are further along your journey of healing, look back at what you have written, and realize how far you have come with your progress.

JOURNAL PROMPT: WRITE AN UNSENT LETTER

Here's your opportunity to tell the toxic person exactly what you think of them and how they made you feel. Let it all out. Before starting this exercise, spend a moment getting comfortable and taking some deep breaths. What would you like to say to the toxic person if he was right in front of you? Or, in a perfect world, what would they say to you to give you a feeling of resolution?

Get it all out. You may prefer to say it out loud to yourself rather than write it, and that is perfectly fine. Try to not criticize, censor, or edit while you are writing. This process of writing freely is called stream-of-consciousness journaling.

Get Comfortable with Ambiguity

Our issue with not getting closure is that it doesn't give the finality that our brain craves. We like making sense of things. If we find a reason why something happened, it is easier for us to digest and accept. But we will never get answers to some of our questions in life; we will never completely know why things happened the way they did. We could spend hours meditating, yelling, praying, Googling, and we still wouldn't have an answer. We will never get an answer that satisfies us. Once you separate yourself from a toxic relationship, you may feel a sense of urgency to not feel what you are feeling and also to understand why the person was toxic. You may feel that patience is just not present in your life. However, sometimes we do gain answers, just not in our own time.

CHECK-IN: ARE YOU OKAY WITH THE UNKNOWN?

When you aren't able to get the closure you want or think you need, it can leave you feeling "stuck." If you are wondering why you aren't able to move forward, it might be that you are having difficulty accepting that you may not receive the answer you want. Answer yes or no to the following statements about accepting ambiguity.

1. I need to have the answers to things.
2. If I don't understand something, I tend to obsess over it.
3. Not having answers makes me feel anxious.

4. When I don't know why something happened, it makes me feel angry and out of control.
5. I will repetitively ask questions until I get an answer that works for me.
6. When I get an answer to something that has been bothering me, it usually isn't good enough.
7. My friends and family have told me that I have issues with letting things go.
8. I can't focus on work when someone is not acting the way I think they should.
9. I will come up with reasons why someone is acting a certain way, even though I don't know why.
10. I will ask for reassurance from someone that they are not upset with me.

If you answered yes to one or more of these statements, you might have issues with letting things be as they are. You may be continually looking for ways to "fix" things. You may also have difficulty self-soothing when you are feeling anxiety.

Consider seeing a mental health professional as we'll cover in Chapter 6. Chapter 7, all about ways to practice self-care, can help you adopt self-soothing strategies to weather discomfort.

Focus on What You Learned

Instead of wondering, "Why did he do this?" ask yourself, "What can I do to improve my life as a result of this experience?" Look at what you have accomplished and learned from this toxic situation. You may have become a more empathic person, built up more resilience to weather life's storms, and may have formed a better connection with the healthy people in your life.

For instance, Tammy realized through therapy and talking with her friends that she wasn't going to get validation or closure from her soon-to-be ex-husband. She also realized that finalizing the divorce still wouldn't make her feel heard. She decided that she would need to get that validation and closure from herself. Tammy realized that the way her husband had behaved during the marriage was a form of closure. Looking back at the verbal and emotional abuse she endured from her husband was her sign that leaving was the right thing to do. Knowing that she had made the right choice for herself and her family helped her heal.

JOURNAL PROMPT: WHAT DID YOU GAIN FROM THIS EXPERIENCE?

While you are healing from a toxic person, it can be difficult to see what positive changes have come about from your experience. You have grown from this experience, even if you feel depressed and anxious right now. Write down what has happened in your life since the toxic person was removed from it. You may have been able to reconnect with trusted family and friends; you may have moved and found a better job. Even if you think the change is a small one, take note of it. Sometimes, the small changes are actually quite significant.

Seek Meaning and Purpose Instead of Happiness

If you are seeking closure to gain some sense of happiness in your life, you may be pursuing an elusive goal. Instead, seek closure to gain meaning and purpose in your life. When we make happiness an end goal of any process, we tend to feel let down. However, when you seek an understanding of the world around you and yourself, the journey and the destination both become worthwhile. Having meaning in your life significantly decreases the chances of having suicidal thoughts and depressive symptoms as you get older.[1] So, when you are seeking resolution after a toxic relationship, focus on what good it will bring to your life rather than focusing on chasing happiness. That's what worked for Erica, whose sisters had been verbally and emotionally abusive to her for all her life.

When Erica blocked contact with her sisters, she felt lost. She wanted her sisters to apologize for their behavior and approached them about owning up to what they had done. However, her sisters told her that she had "always been difficult," and that Erica "was making it up to get attention, as usual." At that point, she knew she needed to permanently distance herself from her sisters so she could have some peace in her life. However, when she cut contact with them, it didn't give her the sense of relief that she was expecting. Erica realized she would need to find new activities and interests to help her build her confidence and in turn help her heal.

Erica was a retired elementary school teacher, and she really missed being around kids. She decided that she would start a weekly story time where she went to each classroom to read out loud to the students. Erica loved seeing the kids' faces light up when she walked in the room and when she used one of her funny voices for the book's characters. Erica found a sense of purpose again, and she knew if she brightened even one child's day it would be enough. Slowly over time the horrible way her sisters treated her faded into the background.

JOURNAL PROMPT: WHAT GIVES YOUR LIFE MEANING?

When we write out our core values and what gives our lives meaning, it can help us rebuild after enduring abuse. When thinking about your core values, consider which of the following are most important to you. You might resonate with one or more of the values on this list, or something else entirely.

- Achievement
- Autonomy
- Balance
- Bravery
- Community
- Compassion
- Creativity
- Fairness
- Faith
- Family
- Fellowship
- Harmony
- Honesty
- Hope
- Independence
- Integrity
- Justice
- Kindness
- Learning
- Optimism
- Patience
- Reliability
- Responsibility
- Self-respect
- Service
- Spirituality
- Transparency
- Trust
- Wisdom

When contemplating what gives your life meaning, think back to the times when you really felt connected to your life's purpose. You might have felt a sense of being "in the zone" while you were engaged in that activity—time flew by. What were you doing when you felt hope for your life? What were you doing when you felt peace and contentment? There are no wrong answers—write down what makes you feel good. Try to center some of your energy on those activities or restart them if it has been a while.

Embrace Your Strong Sense of Justice

If you have a strong sense of justice, it can be even more challenging to understand how someone toxic is not "paying" for their behaviors. You may feel that the court system has let you down. It can be challenging to get closure if you feel that you haven't been heard and that your children's best interests haven't been considered. The fact that you have a strong sense of justice is a good thing—it helps you fight for your rights and those of your children.

If you would like to help improve the system, so others don't have to experience what you did, consider advocacy work or volunteering. See Chapter 10 for more information. Some people have gone back to school and received law degrees or counseling degrees as a result of what they went through in the family courts. Improving your life and the lives of others as a result of your experiences can help give you closure.

Forgiveness

Some believe that to get closure, you need to forgive the people who have wronged you. Society has taught us that to be worthy of forgiveness, the person who has wronged us needs to do some form of confession and repentance, which is supposed to bring about a sense of resolution and finality. However, that would require that a person first admitted that they had wronged someone and then took steps to atone for their behavior. Neither of those things is likely to happen from a toxic person. (I know I've said this before, but it bears repeating because it is so easy to forget!)

Here's a radical thought—you don't need to forgive to move on. It is not a requirement to achieve peace in your life. Some people have done things so heinous and cruel that it is almost impossible to forgive them. Some self-help guides become almost obsessive about the need to forgive. It is more important to focus on how you feel and your process of recovery first instead of focusing on the person that harmed you. It is more important to feel good about yourself and your place in your community rather than experiencing a sense of pressure to forgive.[2] Like many people experience after escaping a toxic relationship, you may just be trying to make it through the day at this point. To be pressured to forgive someone is unconscionable. You left a toxic relationship, in part, to get away from being guilted and shamed. You can forgive if and when you're ready. There is no timetable to the forgiveness process. And if you choose to not forgive at this time or anytime in the future, that is completely okay. You have the right to make your own decisions.

But first, it's worth taking a step back to consider what forgiveness really means. Forgiveness is not about condoning or saying that what someone did was right. You can forgive and still hold that person responsible for his actions. You can forgive and still know that what that person did was terrible and that you believe he should face the consequences. Practicing forgiveness, in whatever manner you see fit, can help you feel more connected to humanity and achieve a greater understanding of your own values, and you may also experience less self-harming behaviors.[3]

If you are blaming yourself at all for getting into or staying in a toxic relationship or situation, it can be very difficult to focus on meaning and embrace your sense of justice. Letting go of guilt and forgiving yourself about this is a critical step toward healing, which we'll discuss in the next chapter.

Dealing with Anger

It is normal to feel anger after the end of a toxic relationship. You may be angry about your ex-partner's behavior; you may be angry toward family and friends that tried to get you back together with your ex; you may be mad at yourself for staying as long as you did. You may want your former partner, friend, or coworker to suffer or have a bad life. You have been hurt, so you want someone to feel the same level of suffering.

Wanting to get even is a normal part of human emotions, especially when you have been hurt deeply. You may expect that getting "even" with a toxic person will finally give you a feeling that justice was served. But trying to get revenge on your ex usually doesn't do anything to them and can cause lifetime consequences for you. In fact, toxic people may feed off the fact that you were thinking of them even months after the relationship ended. Do not give them the satisfaction or that power. Getting revenge is a temporary feeling with possible permanent consequences.

You may get angry at God or another higher power, and you may feel guilty about those feelings. It is perfectly normal and acceptable to be angry with God. It may be helpful for you to talk with your clergy or a mental health professional if you are feeling conflicted about being mad with your higher power. Some counselors specialize in spiritual and religious issues.

Feelings of anger after the ending of a relationship are expected, especially when the relationship was toxic. You may even feel bouts of rage. Being that angry may feel like a foreign emotion to you, but I'll say it again: *These feelings are normal.* It's what you ultimately do with those feelings that matters. If you are coping with depression, sometimes depression is actually anger turned inward. Pain is inevitable after a toxic relationship, but suffering is not.

CHECK-IN: DO YOU HAVE ANGER CONTROL ISSUES?

Answer yes or no to the following statements:

1. I find myself snapping at family and friends.
2. If I feel anger, it is hard to control it.
3. I have lashed out at others through my words and actions.
4. I get so angry that I get physical symptoms, such as a headache or stomachache.

5. Family and friends have told me that I have an anger management problem.

6. I get preoccupied with thoughts of getting even or getting revenge on someone.

7. My anger is out of proportion to events.

8. I have gotten in trouble at work or school due to my anger.

9. I feel that I will always have this feeling of anger.

10. I have turned toward unhealthy ways to stop my anger. (Examples include drinking, over- or undereating, exercising too much, or other unhealthy coping mechanisms listed on page 68.)

If you answered yes to more than one of these statements, I urge you to meet with a mental health professional to talk about your anger. High levels of anger affect not only your relationships but also your physical health. For instance, feeling anger triggers the release of stress hormones throughout the body, increasing heart rate and blood pressure. If anger becomes chronic, elevated levels of those hormones put you at higher risk for heart disease and stroke.[4] For more information on mental health professionals, see Chapter 6.

• • • • •

Seeking closure from a toxic person means that you are opening the door to reconnection with them. The good news is that you don't necessarily need "closure" to go on to have a happy and fulfilled life, and you can achieve resolution on your own.

Don't feel pressured to forgive someone for what they did to you—you might not be ready. It's normal to be angry with a toxic person or situation. You may also be having issues with feeling anger toward yourself. If it's not resolved, that self-directed anger could cause feelings of anxiety and depression, so it's important to take steps to forgive yourself. I know that is sometimes easier said than done! We'll explore why in the next chapter—as well as how to do it.

4

FORGIVE YOURSELF

How to Let Go of Anger and Self-Blame

AFTER LEAVING A TOXIC RELATIONSHIP OR SITUATION, YOU MAY BE FEEL-ing angry toward yourself. You may be mad that you didn't separate yourself from the situation earlier or because you think you "should have known better."

When we harbor resentment and anger toward ourselves, it can impact our relationships with other people and our quality of life. You may have self-hatred that is so deep that you have thought about hurting or killing yourself. You may have resumed or increased self-harm. Although it's normal to feel some level of disappointment toward yourself from time to time, if your sleep, appetite, and general well-being are starting to be affected, it's time to seek some help and do some introspection. When you feel anger toward yourself, it may be challenging to engage in two critical parts of healing—first, learning how you grew from this experience, and second, creating and feeling some sense of justice. When you work on healing anger toward yourself, you can get toward the deeper parts of healing.

As you read this chapter, there are a couple of things I'd like you to keep in mind. First, to paraphrase the physician and author Gerald G.

Jampolsky, remember that forgiveness is the practice of giving up the hope that the past can be any different.

Second, realize that sometimes it can be harder to forgive yourself than it is to forgive someone else. We tend to be more critical of ourselves than we are of others. If you have been in a toxic relationship, this may be especially true. The toxic person most likely blamed you for his behavior and told you that you needed to change. It can take some time to realize that you are worthy of respect, love, and self-compassion.

"I ended up treating myself the way my mother treated me. And that needed to change."

—Alizeh, 25

Practicing self-compassion, or treating yourself like you would a best friend, is one step toward healing. Would you continually tell a best friend that they weren't good enough or don't deserve to be happy? Of course not. You would be loving and supportive toward them. The toxic person in your life most likely didn't show you any compassion, but you can still extend it toward yourself.

CHECK-IN: ARE YOU HAVING DIFFICULTY FORGIVING YOURSELF?

Forgiving yourself can be a multistep process. You may be aware that you are directing anger toward yourself or even being angry at yourself and not realizing it. Let's check in. Do you agree or disagree with the following statements?

1. I feel I have irreparably damaged my relationships with family and friends.
2. I am feeling a tremendous amount of shame and guilt.
3. I feel I could have done things differently, and it eats me up inside.
4. I am dealing with anger toward myself.
5. I feel that I don't have a right to be happy.
6. I don't blame others for being angry with me.
7. I feel I deserve to pay for staying in this relationship too long.
8. I stay awake at night, wondering what I did wrong.
9. I sabotage myself because I don't feel I deserve better.
10. I have negative thoughts about myself consistently.

If you answered yes to one or more of these statements, you might have difficulties forgiving yourself. This chapter explores some common beliefs that can be barriers to self-compassion, as well as actionable steps you can take to move on.

No One Is Immune to Toxic Situations

Part of your anger toward yourself might be that you can't believe how you, a reasonable, put-together adult, fell for a toxic person. You may be kicking yourself that you didn't see the signs of a toxic workplace when you first started working there, or that you tolerated mistreatment from your family for so long.

Be aware that *anyone* can be vulnerable to a toxic person or environment. It doesn't matter how smart or educated you are. It doesn't matter that your past relationships were healthy. Toxic people can sway anyone with love-bombing. It can be virtually impossible to spot the signs of a toxic workplace during a job interview, while you're focused on trying to impress. Unhealthy relationships or situations don't usually start that way—the toxicity builds up over time, like what happened for Sarah at her workplace.

Sarah had looked forward to working for one particular firm since she graduated from college. It was one of the best-regarded companies in her field. Sarah did her research before her interview, and there were no red flags that she noticed. It seemed that people who knew the company held them in high esteem. After nailing her interview, Sarah was offered a reasonable salary and benefits package and excitedly accepted. But on her first day, one of her new coworkers, Sam, stopped by her desk and leaned in a little too close. "I thought you had a right to know this, Sarah," he told her. "Your boss has a history of harassing women at the company." He urged her to let him know if there was any way he could help her.

Sarah was confused. This was a company with a great reputation, and so far her interactions with her new boss had been nothing but professional. If this was a known problem, why wouldn't anyone report his behavior to HR? The whole interaction struck her as very strange.

Nonetheless, Sarah didn't want to be seen as a "complainer," especially not on her first day. So, she dove into her training and kept busy, avoiding Sam as much as possible.

One day she arrived at her cubicle to see that all the items on her desk had been moved—but only by a few inches. Weeks later, Sarah received a notification that someone had tried to log on to one of her work accounts. She reported it to her boss, and an investigation was opened. As part of the process, Sarah started documenting in writing what was happening to her at work: her lunch constantly going missing, Sam taking credit for her work, and being left off team meeting scheduling, even after notifying the team of the error.

A few months later while in the employee restroom, a coworker got in her face and called her a liar. Sarah had seen this coworker on her floor but had no interactions with her up to that point. Shaken, Sarah decided not to tell anyone about it as she was concerned that it would make the situation worse. The next day, Sarah's boss called her into his office and said there was a complaint of theft against her, and she was going to be investigated. When she walked into the break room, her once-friendly coworkers turned their backs to her. Sam walked by her cubicle and said, "You know what you did," and laughed. She decided she would file a harassment claim with HR, and she contacted an attorney that specialized in employment issues. Still, Sarah couldn't stop fixating on the missteps she'd made along the way. She should have reported what happened in the restroom or gone to her boss with Sam's comments on her first day. She felt angry with herself for not seeing red flags and for even taking the job in the first place. Sarah's work performance decreased, and she started having anxiety attacks and insomnia.

Anger as a Form of Anxiety and Fear

When you are angry toward yourself, it may be covering up other feelings. Sometimes, anger is really masking anxiety or fear. Those can be similar feelings, but there are key differences between them.

Anxiety is a sense that something bad is going to happen, but you don't know exactly what it would be. There's a vague but strong sense of foreboding. Sometimes, we feel anxiety when we've pushed down other emotions to avoid feeling them. When we're anxious, it can be very difficult to tell what other emotions are underneath. Fear, in contrast, is an emotion in itself. Fear is a result of seeing, hearing, or sensing danger around you—from an event, person, animal, or thing.

Another difference between anxiety and fear is whether the feeling motivates you to take action. Anxiety can make you feel paralyzed, whereas fear usually motivates a person to move themselves away from a threat. Are you experiencing anxiety, fear, or both?

Talking with a mental health professional (MHP) can help you wade through your emotions, especially after you have exited a toxic relationship. Anxiety can also be controlled or at least reduced through exercise, mindfulness practice, therapy, and medication. You'll learn more about working with an MHP in Chapter 6 and mindfulness in Chapter 7.

JOURNAL PROMPT: LABEL YOUR PHYSICAL REACTIONS

When you are healing from a relationship with a toxic person, you may have physical sensations, such as a racing heartbeat, clammy hands, or a sense of dread. Feeling this way is normal when you have cut ties with someone that is not healthy for you. There is a period of adapting to your new normal. Sometimes, when you are feeling those sensations, it can be difficult to tell if it is anxiety or fear. Draw a stick person in your journal and label the part of the body with the sensation you feel. You can even number them in the order that you feel them. Maybe you tend to get clammy hands first, then it feels as if you can't breathe, then your heart races. Recognizing that those sensations are coming on is half the battle. When you know you are headed into anxiety or fear, quickly practice a self-soothing strategy, such as taking a deep breath or going for a walk. Review the stick figure in another week or two to see whether those sensations have changed for you.

JOURNAL PROMPT: IS IT ANGER, ANXIETY, OR FEAR?

When you are feeling angry, is it a reaction to anxiety or fear? You may be angry toward the toxic person for how they have treated you. That anger may also be a result of anxiety about continuing your life without that person. You may have fear that you will not be able to rebuild, or you may have fear about feeling out of control. Write down what you are thinking and feeling when you are angry. Then, dive deeper and write out what anxiety and fear might be connected to your anger.

The Pervasive Hold of Guilt and Shame

Guilt and shame are two of the most powerful emotions we can have. They can tear us apart and leave us empty. They don't add a lot of positives to our lives. Guilt happens when you perceive that you have violated your moral standards and have done something you shouldn't have done. Shame is an emotion that happens when you are negatively evaluating yourself. It makes you want to hide or be in denial about things that you have done or have happened to you. Feelings of guilt and shame are correlated with depressive symptoms, whereas shame is strongly associated with anxiety.[1]

Guilt and shame can be difficult to let go of, especially if a toxic person used those feelings to manipulate you. You may have heard something like this from a toxic person:

- "If you could just act normal, we wouldn't have a problem."
- "You are an embarrassment to me and the whole family."
- "What is wrong with you?"
- "How dare you be upset with me after all you have done?"
- "Come back to me when you're perfect and then we can talk about my behavior."
- "You have no right to be upset with me."

These are all tactics to divert you from bringing up her inappropriate behaviors. You tell a toxic person that her behavior upset you, and she responds, "You always want too much! What about me? What about how I've suffered? You don't know what I've been through!" The conversation then gets turned around so you look like the bad guy. A toxic person may have told you that, if you didn't do or say something, he wouldn't have reacted that way. You didn't make anyone do anything—you only have control over your actions and perceptions. The toxic person is fully responsible for his behavior. The purpose of guilting and shaming in a toxic relationship is to "keep you in line" and exert control over you.

If you start to feel that you deserve to be punished or treated poorly, the toxic person will run with that and ramp up the guilt and shame. You may find yourself using the words *would, could,* and *should* when you are feeling guilt or shame. Examples are

- "I should have known better."
- "I should call my parents."
- "I could have done more."
- "I could be better if I really tried."
- "I would leave, but I don't know how."
- "I would have helped her, but I didn't know she needed it."

All these statements are things I've heard from my clients either in or after a toxic situation. If you're thinking, *I should have known better,* please forgive yourself for not picking up on the signs earlier. Remember, people who gaslight or have narcissistic behavior are very, very good at covering up their destructive behaviors and they tend to look great on paper, especially during the idealizing phase of the relationship. They are also very good at blaming their behavior on others.

If you're telling yourself, "I could have left earlier," or "I never should have gone back," I'd encourage you to revisit Chapter 1 and remember that there are reasons that good, smart, reasonable people end up in toxic relationships. The toxic person may have used emotional blackmail or threats to keep you in the relationship. It may be that the cycle of escalation, abuse, remorse, and rebuilding resulted in trauma bonding, which makes it harder to leave or cut off contact with an abusive person. You also most likely experienced cognitive dissonance during the toxic relationship. Cognitive dissonance can throw you for a loop, and it can be challenging to make decisions while experiencing it—sapping your emotional or mental energy to leave the situation. It can be helpful to examine how guilt and shame contribute to how you are feeling, such as with the "Letting Go of Guilt and Shame" journal prompt on page 65 and with the help of your trusted MHP (more on that in Chapter 6).

"I had a lot of guilt for leaving my younger siblings at home with my mother when I went off to college. My therapist told me I had a right to start a life for myself."

—Bonnie, 64

"I spent years beating myself up for not leaving sooner. I realize now that I was being manipulated into thinking I could never survive on my own."

—Ingrid, 40

The bottom line is that it is difficult to leave a toxic situation, and for reasons beyond your control. The important thing is that you have left, and that is a courageous thing to do.

Stop Gaslighting Yourself

You may have told yourself, *"but I was also abusive"* toward a partner or a member of your family. Remember, there is a thing called reactive abuse (see page 12). This is when you are backed into a corner or relentlessly mocked, and you fight back as a form of survival. It does not mean *you* are abusive.

Telling yourself that you were also abusive is kind of like gaslighting yourself. It may save you from looking at the other person's pattern of abuse, but it is also a form of denial. It may be helpful to talk to a mental health professional about what you have experienced and your conflicted feelings about your behavior in the relationship. You are worthy of self-forgiveness.

"I eventually started yelling back at her. I'm not even a yeller. She turned me into someone I didn't recognize. Then she would tell me I was irrational and out of control."

—Aydin, 35

JOURNAL PROMPT: LETTING GO OF GUILT AND SHAME

In your journal, write down the self-talk that relates to feeling guilt and shame. Identify where that self-talk comes from. Is it something you heard from your parents, a teacher, a boss, or a partner? Then, write a sentence that reverses that guilt and shame. For example, "You can't do anything right" can be changed to "I am always doing the best I can, and that is enough" or "I have succeeded in many areas of my life." Whenever you catch yourself with negative self-talk around guilt and shame, turn to your journal and rewrite that narrative. After a while, you'll find yourself automatically turning negative self-talk into positives.

Having to Leave Pets

Your former partner may have owned a pet that you became attached to, or you and your partner may have adopted a pet together. So, you may have had an extra layer of heartbreak leaving the relationship. Many times animals can distinguish between a toxic person and a healthy one—and you may have become that pet's favorite person. Although it is usually in the pet's best interest to go with the healthier person, that's not always possible. You may have moved to a place where pets weren't allowed. Your ex may have promised that you could see your shared pet regularly, but she didn't follow through. Or you may have decided that your mental health was worth not having contact with her again to see the pet.

Leaving your pet can be one of the most stressful experiences about ending a toxic relationship. You may be angry with yourself for "abandoning" your pet. Sometimes, life gives us tough choices. It is time to forgive yourself. You are doing the best you can, and your pet will remember the good times you shared.

"Leaving Lulu with my ex was one of the hardest things I have ever done. She was his dog, but we got really attached to each other. I wanted to see her again, but I knew that would mean having contact with him that would send me in a downward spiral."

—Jane, 28

Cultivate an Internal Locus of Control

Lauren decided it was time to move out of her parents' house. Years of emotional and verbal abuse had taken a toll on her—her parents had always blamed her for anything that went wrong in their home life, and she felt that she couldn't do anything right. Lauren moved in with her partner of a few years. While they had a mostly healthy relationship, she didn't feel comfortable bringing up issues because she wanted to avoid confrontation as much as possible. She had experienced enough yelling and fighting at home—she didn't want to potentially set him off, even though he had never displayed any issues with anger. She was also afraid that if she brought up any issues, her partner would dump her and she would have to return to her parents' house. If her partner or friends did something that upset her, or anyone said anything critical to her, it would change her whole mood. One day, her partner suggested—kindly—that she might benefit from going to a counseling session.

When Lauren met with the counselor, the counselor asked her what her mood was on a scale of 1 to 10, with 1 being a really bad mood, and 10 being a really great mood. "I'm at a 7 right now," Lauren responded, "but I could go anywhere from a 2 to a 9 depending on what happens today."

"What changes your mood?" Lauren's counselor asked. When Lauren described the events that would usually bring her down, her counselor asked if her mood tended to depend on what happened around her.

"Of course, how could it not?" Lauren replied. So, her counselor introduced her to the concept of having an *external locus of control.*

When you have an external locus of control, things happen to you, and your mood changes based on the situation. If you are in a bad mood, it is difficult for you to take yourself out of it. In contrast, when you have an *internal locus of control,* you feel solid and grounded. Things happen to you, and they may impact your mood somewhat, but you can let them bounce off you. You feel that you can handle most things because you look inward to find strength and resilience.

Lauren and her counselor talked about her experiences with her parents and how they changed the ways she interacted with her partner and friends. Lauren's moods tended to be very dependent on other people's behaviors. Over the course of several weeks, Lauren's counselor helped her shift to an internal locus of control, where Lauren felt pretty calm and knew that other people's behavior toward her was not personal—in other words, she could forgive herself and not feel responsible for everyone else around her. Lauren was able to really listen to what her partner and her friends were saying, without getting defensive or falling into a bad mood. Lauren started talking openly about what she needed from her relationship and her friendships without fearing abandonment or arguments, and it changed her life for the better.

When you haven't forgiven yourself, you tend to let external forces shape how you feel and behave. When you forgive yourself, you are moving more toward having an internal locus of control. Loving yourself means moving more toward trusting yourself and knowing that you will be okay.

Of course, trusting yourself and treating yourself well are easier said than done. But through the following practices of self-compassion, you can move actively toward this goal.

Practices of Self-Compassion

Letting go of what is holding you down can be a very liberating process. You deserve to be happy and free of guilt and shame. These practices of self-compassion are essential when working on forgiving yourself and letting go of emotions that don't serve you.

Affirmations

Although affirmations may seem silly or untrue, many times, if we repeat something to ourselves enough, it becomes so. That can be true whether you are speaking to yourself negatively or positively. You may have negative "recordings" in your self-talk. For example, you may hear the voice of your ex-partner or a family member telling you that you aren't good enough or worse. Try using an affirmation to counteract negative self-talk. You can come up with your own affirmations or use one of the affirmations provided here.

"I am calm, cool, and collected."

"I am healthy and well."

"Today is full of miracles."

A tip when creating affirmations: keep them positive. Eliminate *don't*, *can't*, or similar words. Your affirmations can be whatever makes you feel hopeful and content. Put your affirmation as your lock screen on your phone, and post it in places you go to frequently in your home, such as on your refrigerator or bathroom mirror. You can even have timed pop-ups on your phone with your affirmation. Notice how you seem to have a more positive outlook during the day when you are using affirmations. Remember, you don't even really need to believe the affirmation for it to work.

Turn to Positive Coping Strategies

After leaving your toxic situation, you may have found that you have gotten into some bad habits. Part of that might be the result of finally being able to do whatever you want without being ridiculed or manipulated. However, you might be engaging in high-risk behaviors to feel something other than anger or sadness—what therapists refer to as *maladaptive coping*. Ask yourself whether you notice yourself doing any of the following to cope:

- Increased alcohol or drug use
- Engaging in high-risk sexual behaviors, such as having unprotected sex with multiple partners
- Misusing prescription drugs
- Avoiding time with healthy friends and family
- Eating too much or too little
- Exercising too much
- Self-injury
- Increased risk-taking
- Significantly increased time online

You may not be fully aware of how these unhealthy coping mechanisms are affecting you. But over time you may find that they increase your stress levels, wear you down, and are harmful to your health and mental well-being. These unhealthy coping strategies won't help you actively work toward healing—in fact, just the opposite, making them a form of self-sabotage. If you're engaging in these behaviors, it may be due to deep-seated issues with self-worth.

Positive coping strategies, on the other hand, keep you grounded in the present and can help you work toward solutions to your feelings of anger, sadness, and low self-worth. Not every strategy will work for everyone; pick one or a few that appeal to you and keep trying new ones until you find something that helps you. Here are some ideas:

> *"I found that even though I fought against becoming an alcoholic like my father, I started to not be able to control my drinking. I realized that I was using drinking to cover up feelings of anger toward myself. With the help of a therapist and a recovery program, I've been sober for two years. Now when I get frustrated, I journal or talk to my spouse or a friend."*
>
> —Caterina, 32

- Making time to see a friend
- Taking a soothing bath or shower
- Doing something creative, such as drawing, writing, or playing a musical instrument
- Playing with your kids
- Spending time playing with your pets
- Getting outdoors to spend some time in nature
- Any of the self-care practices described in Chapter 7—for instance, getting good sleep, practicing meditation, journaling, doing moderate exercise, and/or limiting social media use

If you are struggling, talking with a mental health professional can help you sort through your feelings, help you decrease maladaptive coping, and increase healthy ways to take care of yourself. (For more information on mental health professionals, see Chapter 6.)

Reframe Negative Thoughts and Let Go of *Should*

You may be telling yourself that you "should have left sooner," "shouldn't have taken that job," or "should have seen this coming." When you use the word *should*, it puts a lot of pressure on you. We can't change the past, so using *should* puts you in a no-win situation. The same idea applies when using *could have* or *would have*. These phrases don't propel you forward—they can get you stuck in a rut. As you read earlier in this chapter, using *would*, *could*, and *should* can be related to feelings of guilt and shame.

> "I used to tell myself I should have left earlier and that I should have seen the signs that my boss was toxic. I realized that he was able to act 'normal' in the beginning, and there's no way I could have known what he was really like."
>
> —Eduardo, 45

Catch yourself using *should*, *would*, and *could*, and rephrase it into a positive instead. For example, "I should have left earlier" can be changed into "I left when I did, and that's okay." Reframing negative thoughts can help give you hope for the future and just make you feel better. The more you practice canceling out negative thoughts and reframing them as positives, the easier it gets. You may even notice your total amount of negative thoughts has dramatically decreased with time. Here are some examples of negative thoughts and how you can reframe them:

THOUGHT	REFRAMED
"I don't know how I'm going to make it through this."	"I'm going through a challenging time right now, but it will get better. I have ways I can reach out for help."
"I can't believe I was so stupid and didn't see earlier on that she was a narcissist."	"Narcissists can be difficult to spot, and I had the courage to leave."
"I don't know if I can trust anyone again."	"It may be difficult at first for me to trust others, but I will get there."
"I would do anything to get him back in my life."	"It's good that I am no longer with him, I am sleeping better, and I'm getting healthier each day."

"I must have done something to make my boss harass me."	"Harassment is fully the fault of the harasser; I did nothing that warranted that behavior."
"I don't have anyone to reach out to."	"I have more support than I may realize right now."

Share Your Experiences

Many people don't talk about their experiences with toxic people, due to guilt and shame, but you are not alone. Recently, more people are talking openly about being survivors of abuse and harassment, in part due to the #MeToo movement. Sometimes, when we speak out about wrongs that have been done toward us, it gives us a feeling of freedom. It is a lifting of guilt and shame. When guilt and shame leave you, many times, anger leaves along with them.

"I found a 12-step group for people who grew up in dysfunctional families. I go to a meeting every week. It's really good to know there are other people who experienced the same things that I did, and they don't judge me."

—Katya, 30

Speak out about your experiences in whatever way feels safe to you. That could be done in therapy, in a support group, face-to-face with trusted friends and family, or online, such as on a blog.

One caveat here: Check with a legal professional to learn the boundaries of what you can or can't disclose about your experience with a toxic person or situation. For example, using a person's name and labeling them as a toxic person may get you into legal trouble, whereas you may be able to discuss what you have experienced as long as you don't give identifying details.

Another way you can speak out is by advocating for others who have survived toxic people and experiences. For example, you can advocate for changes in laws regarding protections for victims of domestic violence. You can also educate younger people about identifying healthy versus unhealthy people. For more information on advocating for others, see Chapter 10.

Stop Second-Guessing Yourself

When you leave a harmful situation, you may be second-guessing yourself. You may wonder if the abuse was really as bad as you remembered. You may tell yourself that maybe you were overexaggerating by thinking a person's behavior was harmful.

When you are venturing out on your own and rebuilding after abuse, it is normal to feel like you may have made a mistake. This is usually your fear talking—the abusive relationship or situation was harmful to you, but striking out on your own is full of uncertainties. You may get angry with yourself that you have considered returning to a situation that was unhealthy because at least it was predictable. You would not have left the relationship or environment if it was healthy. You made the right decision by leaving. If a toxic person left you, consider that she did you a favor. The situation you were in would have gotten more dangerous with time. Acknowledge your need for certainty and stability. That day is coming. There will be a point when you feel less discomfort and more of a sense of being grounded and centered.

JOURNAL PROMPT: WHAT HAS GONE WELL FOR YOU?

When you second-guess yourself about detaching from a toxic person, you may forget the good things that have happened to you since you broke contact. Take a moment to write down the opportunities you have had, the people you have met, and any improvements in your health and general outlook on life since you last had contact with the toxic person. You have probably had a cascade of positive things happen once you got the toxic person or situation out of your life. It can be difficult to see the good events when you are feeling anxious or down. However, you probably have more time now to pursue interests and focus on what brings you happiness. Continue writing down the good events in your life as they happen. When you are feeling like you made a mistake in distancing from the toxic person, go back and review this list of the good things that have happened to you since then.

• • • • •

After your toxic relationship ends, it is normal for you to have feelings of anger and resentment toward others and yourself. You may also feel guilt or shame. *These are all normal feelings*, and no one is immune from toxic situations. When you can let go of feeling responsible for your experience, you'll be able to cultivate an internal locus of control, giving you resilience that extends into all your relationships and helps you weather life's ups and downs. Another key step to building up your resilience is setting and maintaining healthy boundaries. That's where we're headed next.

5

ESTABLISH BOUNDARIES

How to Protect Your Interests and Put Yourself First

L OOKING BACK AT HIS YOUNGER YEARS, RHYS DESCRIBES HIMSELF AS A quiet child who didn't want to cause trouble. It was mostly just Rhys and his dad, and a variety of people who would drift in and out of the house. While he has difficulty remembering parts of his childhood due to trauma he endured, he clearly recalls the chaos around his father's opiate addiction. Sometimes, his dad let his "friends" abuse Rhys, physically and sexually, in exchange for drugs. His dad had told him that if he talked about his family at school, he would be taken away from home—and went on to describe the terrible things that would happen to Rhys if the state took him. Sometimes, Rhys hoped that his teachers would notice that he needed help because that way maybe his dad wouldn't blame him when they found out. Other times, he remembered that his dad wasn't always high—there were times that he acted maybe how other dads do. But he didn't really know how other dads acted because he didn't socialize much with other kids.

Years later, Rhys felt he owed his survival to his partner, Odette, who gave him a place to live when he left his dad's house and cut off contact. However, when Rhys went out, Odette wanted to know where he was going and when he was coming back, and would message and call him repeatedly. When Rhys tried to talk to Odette about her behavior, she lashed out: "I rescued you from an abusive home, Rhys—I'm just trying to look out for you. How ungrateful can you be?"

Rhys recently struck up a friendship with a coworker, Ben. As Rhys and Ben got to know each other, it turned out that they had similar childhoods and experiences. Ben had done a lot of work to heal from his trauma. One day as they walked together on their lunch break, Ben gently brought up Odette. "You've tried to talk to her about this a few times now," he said. "But it's just not possible to have a healthy relationship with somebody who won't take responsibility for her behavior."

"I don't even know what a healthy relationship looks like," Rhys admitted. "I mean, I know the way she's acting isn't right. But I feel as if I'm overreacting sometimes, especially when I think about how stuff was with my dad. At least Odette cares where I am and what I'm doing."

"I really think you need to do some work here," Ben said. "Process what you went through as a kid and learn to set boundaries." Rhys had heard the term *boundaries* but wasn't really sure what it meant. Ben said that having good boundaries helped him set healthy limits with people as to how he expected to be treated. "It's hard at first, man," he said, "but the more I got used to enforcing my boundaries, the more I had healthy people in my life."

What Are Boundaries?

Boundaries are guidelines or limits that you place on yourself and your relationships. They are a way of making sure that you protect your own well-being and don't put others' needs ahead of your own. There are different types of boundaries:

1. **Emotional boundaries** are about honoring your feelings and your energy, knowing when is the right time to share (and how much to share), and recognizing how much emotional energy you can handle.

2. **Physical boundaries** are about maintaining personal space, your comfort level with being touched, and making sure your body's needs (e.g., food, water, and sleep) are met. They also include exercising within a range that is healthy for your body.

3. **Sexual boundaries** are about engaging in sexual activity only with your and your partners' consent, communicating to your partners the sexual activities in which you are and aren't interested, and having the right to change your mind or say no to any activity in which you feel uncomfortable or unsafe.

4. **Time boundaries** are about knowing your priorities and setting aside time for them without overcommitting yourself, and saying no to requests that are not a wise use of your time.

5. **Mental boundaries** are about respect for thoughts and ideas— your own and others'. Having these boundaries means being willing to discuss issues respectfully, and expecting the same from the person with whom you are engaged in dialogue. They also include your right to seek out information and become educated in areas of interest and concern.

You may have found in toxic relationships that you weren't sure what your rights were or that the other person seemed to challenge your boundaries consistently.

In this chapter, you'll learn about healthy boundaries, your rights as a person, how attachment style influences our boundaries, and ways to maintain boundaries in specific situations, such as coparenting. Healthy boundaries include

- Saying no to things that don't fit in your life or that make you uncomfortable or unsafe
- Saying yes to support or help
- Telling others when you need time alone—and taking it
- Having interests outside your relationship
- Expressing yourself with open communication

- Letting others know your boundaries
- Letting others know, directly and assertively, when a boundary has been crossed
- Enjoying yourself without guilt or shame
- Stating what you want and need
- Being able to identify unhealthy behaviors in others
- Being vulnerable in a relationship in steps or stages
- Accepting transitions and changes
- Being aware of what you have control over and what you don't have control over

"It's amazing how much easier my life is now that I'm not in a relationship with an asshole."

—Caroline, 54

You'll also learn how much time and energy you get back in your life when your brain space isn't taken up by a toxic person.

Boundaries can change over time, and some may be more flexible than others. For example, expressing your boundaries to others may be most important to you, while "having interests outside your relationship" may not be as important to you if you and the other person share many of the same passions and hobbies. As you read this chapter, think about which boundaries are most important to you right now.

If someone has crossed a boundary with you, it is up to you to either clearly draw that line or decide if that person has a place in your life. If there is not a way to distance yourself from that person (such as a co-parent), it might be time to reassess limiting contact with that person as much as possible.

JOURNAL PROMPT: WRITE OUT YOUR BOUNDARIES

The toxic person in your life tried to dismantle or ignore your boundaries, so you may have the mistaken belief that you don't have any. You probably have more boundaries established than you think. To identify them, reflect: What are the rules by which you guide your life? What are the things or people in your life that you would fight to protect? What would you tell someone are the values you live by?

Some examples of boundaries are
- I will be treated with respect.
- I will be spoken to in a respectful tone.
- I don't lend money out to friends, family, or partners.

If you are having difficulty coming up with your boundaries, it's okay. Think of someone that you look up to, living or dead. What are or were the rules they led their life by? Consider taking those on as your boundaries.

Write down your boundaries and review them regularly. Having a written reminder of your boundaries is especially helpful when you meet someone you are interested in, get a gut feeling something isn't right in your life, or are making big decisions. These are times you might be tempted to let your boundaries slide—and the written record will help you stay accountable to yourself.

JOURNAL PROMPT: COPING WITH A BOUNDARY VIOLATION

Think back to when you told someone, verbally or nonverbally, that how they were treating you was not okay. Did they respect your boundary? Or were they taken aback or even offended? Enforcing a boundary might have been outside your comfort zone. You may have been "punished" by someone because you enforced your boundary.

The idea of enforcing a boundary may cause feelings of anxiety or a sense of bewilderment. Remember, you have the right to enforce or restate a boundary any time you want, for any reason. This journal entry is about how you felt about setting a boundary, the reaction you received, and how that shapes your ability to enforce boundaries today. Write down in as much detail as possible

> *what happened when you set a boundary. Now write what you would have liked to have happened instead. You are writing a new ending to the story and taking back control of the narrative.*

How to Enforce Boundaries

A toxic person might tell you that your boundaries are silly or ridiculous or that you are too sensitive. Your experiences in the relationship may have taught you that establishing boundaries was a sign of weakness or that you didn't know how to enforce boundaries.

The truth is, you have had the power to enforce boundaries. You were just told you didn't have a right to. The upside here is that you probably already have lots of experience with upholding boundaries even if it was difficult in the toxic situation. Think back. Including since childhood, have you ever done the following?

- Told anyone no
- Told anyone no and didn't feel the need to provide an explanation
- Stuck up for someone who was being bullied or harassed
- Told someone what you needed
- Wrote an email to a company or called them when your order was incorrect
- Returned an item to the store
- Invited people to a social event
- Set limits with your child
- Stopped yourself from checking messages, emails, and voicemail after a certain time
- Backed away when someone touched your hair, tattoo, scar, or pregnant belly without asking
- Said no to any sales call, hung up, or refused to answer
- Told a doctor about your reaction to treatment or that your symptoms weren't going away

- Noticed someone performing a task incorrectly and notified them or showed them how to do it
- Taught children
- Were a supervisor of someone
- Reviewed someone's work
- Sent food back at a restaurant because it tasted bad, was the wrong order, or was undercooked
- Made decisions about a child's, parent's, or pet's health

Those are all examples of setting and holding a boundary. You've done it before and I know you can do it again.

Your Rights as a Person

In addition to your boundaries, you also have rights as a human being. You have the right to

- Feel safe
- Say no at any time
- Change your mind at any time
- Choose with whom you spend your time
- Do less than what is humanly possible
- Be treated with respect
- Make your own decisions

When your rights have been violated, that can create an even bigger issue than a crossed boundary. Look at your rights as your "line in the sand." If someone steps on your rights, that might mean automatic disqualification from being in your life. If you don't feel safe with someone, that is not negotiable. Listen to that gut feeling that says that something is wrong.

"I had a hard time saying no to people, especially because I didn't want to disappoint them. If I did say no to someone, I would go into an explanation as to why I was saying no, and then I would worry afterward that the person was upset with me. Then I heard someone say, 'No is a complete sentence,' and that made me realize that I didn't have to explain why I said no. I have the right to just say no, and that's it."

—Bailey, 32

CHECK-IN: HOW ARE YOUR BOUNDARIES?

For the following statements, answer yes or no to whether you use these boundaries *most of the time*. (It's not expected for you to be using these boundaries all the time—we are imperfect people, constantly growing and evolving.)

1. I say no when I am asked to participate in something I don't want to do.
2. If I need help with something, I ask someone.
3. If a friend asks to borrow money and I don't feel comfortable doing so, I say no.
4. If I need some alone time, I let others know without feeling guilty.
5. When I am tired, I rest instead of forcing myself to keep working.
6. If my needs aren't being met in a relationship, I state what I need calmly and respectfully.
7. When I feel I am getting angry, I stop and decide whether I need to take a time-out.
8. If someone is raising their voice, I tell them it makes me uncomfortable, and I need them to stop.
9. I can accept a compliment with a simple "thank you."
10. I am aware of my strengths and weaknesses.
11. If I feel that I am being misunderstood, I discuss it with the other person.
12. If someone is upset, I don't feel that I need to fix the issue.

If you answered yes to more than half these statements, you have reasonably healthy boundaries. Pay attention to the items you answered no to, and work on improving those.

If you answered no to a majority of these statements, focus on improving your boundaries one at a time.

Attachment Styles

Your ability to maintain healthy boundaries in relationships may be, in part, determined by your *attachment style*. Your attachment style is formed in childhood depending on how your caregivers interacted with you. There are four main attachment styles—anxious, avoidant, disorganized, and secure. The anxious, avoidant, and disorganized attachment styles are known as insecure attachments.

Anxious Attachment

The anxious attachment style is characterized by "I'm not okay, you're okay." This person may have had unpredictable parents or caregivers—there was a push-pull dynamic where the parent intermittently treated the child well and then pushed her away. The main fears underlying this style are abandonment and not being "good enough." She may be unfairly labeled as "needy" or "clingy" and tends to push for *emotional intimacy* quickly.

When dating, she may be preoccupied with thoughts of whether someone is interested in her or if her partner will end the relationship. If a partner doesn't initiate contact, she may become obsessive about why he hasn't been in touch. She may call or text her partner repeatedly to help decrease her feelings of anxiety.

A person with anxious attachment tends to repress concerns about the relationship or express them angrily or via passive-aggressive behavior. She may forgo her boundaries to keep the other person happy and in the relationship. In the workplace, an employee with anxious attachment may obsessively worry that she is not a good enough employee and will be fired at any minute. An email from her boss will lead her to think the worst. She may seek reassurance from others that the work she is producing is adequate.

What other people say and do to a person with anxious attachment is taken very personally. She will wonder what she did to upset her friend or family member, even if the other person was in the wrong. A person with anxious attachment may not consider leaving a situation, even if it's toxic, because being

"I tend to text my friends way too often. I get so anxious if I haven't heard from someone. I immediately wonder what I did to upset them, and then I think about them never wanting to talk to me again. But I've learned that sometimes people are just busy, you know?"

—Lara, 29

alone seems like a worse fate. She may find one friend with whom she is especially attached and then become upset when that friend can't get together.

Avoidant Attachment

The avoidant attachment style is characterized by "I'm okay, you're not okay." A person with avoidant attachment may have had parents or care-takers who didn't provide emotional intimacy, teaching him instead that feelings needed to be stuffed down and not expressed. Avoidant attachment is based on a fear of rejection and being vulnerable in front of another person.

A person with avoidant attachment may have rigid boundaries that don't allow for any changes in personalities or circumstances; he will not bring up concerns in a relationship because he feels that no good would come of it anyway. He may go through a series of relationships that are exciting in the beginning when things are more superficial, but when true emotional intimacy starts he distances himself. A person with this style tends to shy away from physical closeness, such as avoiding holding hands, snuggling, or giving a hug. He may be described as "emotionally distant," "cold," or "aloof." This person may say that he is too busy with work or other activities rather than spend time with his partner, friends, or family. He is highly critical of others and can have perfectionistic tendencies. He can be independent to a fault and has difficulty asking for support.

"I'm working on having avoidant attachment. I have kept my relationships long-distance because otherwise I feel smothered by the other person. I also don't like defining relationships and I hate the 'exclusivity' talk."

—Erik, 50

A person with avoidant attachment may view others as being "less than" and may not take their requests seriously. He tends to avoid family get-togethers or social events because there is too much contact with others and he doesn't want to talk about his life. He can go weeks without contacting someone or spending time with other people but may still feel a sense of loneliness.

Disorganized Attachment

Disorganized attachment is characterized by "I'm not okay, you're not okay." Someone with this attachment style tends to have a severe lack of coping skills. There is both a fear of being abandoned and a fear of being vulnerable with others—a blend of the anxious and avoidant styles, which can be a result of early trauma or abuse. She can have frequent mood changes and feels powerless to change her life circumstances. Forming healthy coping mechanisms can be difficult for her, and she may have erratic behavior, outbursts of anger, self-injurious behavior, or a poor self-image.

A relationship is very difficult to maintain with this attachment style. People with disorganized attachment may have little to no boundaries and may react with anger when a partner states her own limits. A person with disorganized attachment may swing between being overly attached and then distant. It is difficult for friends, family, and colleagues to know where they stand with her.

"I had a disorganized attachment style. I would blow up at a friend for not going somewhere with me but then get anxious that I hadn't heard from her afterward."

—River, 30

Secure Attachment

The secure attachment style is characterized by "I'm okay, you're okay." A person with a secure attachment style feels comfortable being emotionally vulnerable in a relationship and is okay with being on his own. When he has a concern in a relationship, he addresses it honestly and respectfully. He doesn't blame people—he knows that others' behaviors and actions won't always be in alignment with his. He practices good self-care and knows when he needs social contact or time alone.

People with secure attachment tend to have healthy boundaries and are comfortable stating them. They also adjust their boundaries as they and their relationships change. They are willing to walk away from a relationship, friendship, or job in which their needs are not being met. If someone ends a relationship with him, he grieves but doesn't blame himself or attempt to get that person back.

When both people in a relationship have a secure attachment style, they tend to have *interdependence*: each person feels they can be an individual, yet they are comfortable sharing themselves with the other. Each person feels that they are respected and can disagree about something yet still maintain their close bond. Topics that are sensitive to one will be treated with respect by the other.

The Anxious-Avoidant Relationship

In a toxic relationship, it's common to see one partner with anxious attachment and the other with avoidant attachment. Does this sound familiar to you? As soon as you met this person, you may have experienced a feeling of instant attraction or intense sexual chemistry—because you were each filling a particular need. By being "clingy," an anxious person confirms the avoidant partner's belief that being in a relationship means losing independence and identity. In turn, the avoidant person's "aloof" demeanor confirms the anxious person's belief that he is not good enough for other people. In the anxious-avoidant relationship, the avoidant person will take steps to back away from the relationship, while the anxious person will pursue her.

"I used to have what I would call a secure attachment style. However, I was in a relationship with a narcissist, and it made my anxious attachment style pop out. Part of my healing is to get back to a more secure style."

—Meghan, 46

Pay Attention to How You Communicate

If you have an insecure attachment style, you may rely more on communicating through text than through phone calls or face-to-face interactions.[1] An avoidant person may use texting more frequently because it is less emotionally intimate and requires less support from a partner. An anxious person may text more to avoid feelings of abandonment by keeping their partner "close." As texting increases, other forms of communication decrease, and there is a higher level of dissatisfaction in a relationship.[2]

That's not to say that texting can't provide a positive benefit to a relationship. One study found that texting a positive statement to a partner, written in one's own words, positively affected relationship satisfaction. Initiating a text also had a positive effect.[3] It appears that the best way to text is to do so occasionally and only to either state positives or short factual information (e.g., "I'll be there in 10 minutes").

That said, an emotional conversation should not be conducted via text. It does not convey the tone and feeling behind the words, and you miss out on key nonverbal cues, such as facial expression and body language. Meet face-to-face or talk over the phone to help build emotional intimacy and discuss sensitive topics.

> "I am seeing someone with what I think is a secure attachment style. We text each other twice a day max and then talk on the phone every few days. We talked ahead of time about the amount of contact that we both preferred in a new relationship, and this works for both of us."
>
> —Grace, 32

CHECK-IN: WHAT'S YOUR ATTACHMENT STYLE?

Answer yes or no to the following statements about your attachment style.

1. I tend to stuff my feelings down and don't talk about them.
2. If I feel someone has distanced himself from me, I react with anger or refuse to communicate.
3. I don't necessarily need regular contact from my partner, family, or friends.
4. If I don't hear from someone within a certain amount of time, I get anxious.
5. If my partner left, I would move on with relatively little sadness.
6. I am constantly in fear that my partner or a friend will end the relationship.
7. Being affectionate with my partner or my children is not high on my list of needs.
8. I naturally tend to reach out to touch others, and it helps me feel close to them.
9. I am uncomfortable with sustained physical contact with others, including having them sit too close to me.
10. Sometimes, I need to have people near me, or else I feel anxious.

If you mainly answered yes to statements 1, 3, 5, 7, and 9, you might have an avoidant attachment style.

If you mainly answered yes to statements 2, 4, 6, 8, and 10, you may have an anxious attachment style.

If you answered no to most of these statements, you might have a secure attachment style.

You Know Your Attachment Style—Now What?

Now that you have discovered your attachment style, what should you do with that information? If you've realized that you have an insecure attachment style, I want to reassure you that that is not a bad thing—your attachment style is simply a way to explain how you relate to others. Once you know your style, you can become aware of how it impacts your relationships and your choices in friends and partners. You may find that your relationships have had a particular pattern—you might have recognized yourself in some of the descriptions and quotes on the previous pages. Or, if you usually have a secure attachment style, being with an anxious or avoidant person may have brought out some of your own anxious or avoidant behaviors.

Just because you developed a specific attachment style, that doesn't mean that you are destined to have it forever! When you are aware of these patterns, you can start working toward moving to a secure attachment style. You also become more aware of others' attachment styles and understand why they may behave certain ways—and you can make more informed decisions about how much time and energy you would like to spend in that relationship.

The first step toward healing an insecure attachment style is to acknowledge and own it.

Next, learn coping strategies for your attachment style. You may find that your attachment style has impacted not only your romantic relationships but also your relationships with coworkers, family, and friends. A therapist can help you discover the origin of your attachment style, which allows you to heal that hurt and move past it.

If you have a secure attachment style, you may still want to check in with a mental health professional to keep that attachment style intact and working. You may also want to look at whether the relationships in your life have brought out anxious or avoidant tendencies.

We'll cover working with mental health professionals in the next chapter. If you're not currently working with a mental health professional you trust or you want to work on this independently, the rest of this chapter shares ways you can cope with your attachment style on your own.

Coping Strategies for Insecure Attachment Styles

When you have identified your attachment style, try one of the following suggestions for moving toward a secure style.

Strategies for Anxious Attachment

1. Practice mindfulness meditation. Focus on the here and now.
2. If you have not heard from your partner or friend, sit with your anxiety. What are your concerns?
3. Visualize what it would be like if this relationship ended. Know that you would be upset for a while, but you would also eventually be okay.
4. Be aware that what someone says or does is not personal—it is a reflection of them.
5. Become aware of self-sabotaging behaviors such as pushing people away so you don't experience perceived abandonment.
6. Be aware that you are likely to experience negative bias, or attributing negative expectations, ahead of an event. You assume the email you just received will be a negative one, or the voicemail on your phone will tell you terrible news. Practice thought-stopping behaviors: remind yourself that you really don't know the content of the message until you open it or listen to it.

Strategies for Avoidant Attachment

1. Allow yourself to feel emotions instead of avoiding them. It may feel very uncomfortable at first. However, feeling "icky" emotions is part of the human experience.

2. Remind yourself that with significant risk comes great reward. Take a chance on opening up with a partner or trusted friend or family member about a concern you are having. Consider others' feelings when making decisions.

3. Practice being more physically affectionate with your partner or children.

4. Work on returning calls and texts from emotionally healthy people in a timely manner. Acknowledge when you are pulling away from a person who has reasonable expectations for communication and emotional intimacy.

5. Instead of avoiding communication, start with an open-ended question. Open-ended questions are those that can be answered with more than one word. For example, "What did you do today?" is an open-ended question that invites conversation, while "How are you?" is not as inviting.

6. Admit that others can also have valid opinions and may even have more information than you do.

If you have a disorganized attachment style, items from both the anxious and avoidant attachment lists may be helpful. Becoming more anxious or avoidant can happen when you are with an unhealthy or abusive person. The important thing is that you identify it and work on getting to a secure attachment style.

Being on High Alert

After getting out of a toxic situation, you may experience some feelings of *hypervigilance*—that you are on "red alert," looking for signs that anyone new you meet, or any other person around you, is unhealthy. This can be especially true if you are starting to date again.

Sometimes, when we are stretching outside our comfort zone, we can feel awkward, tense, or self-conscious. This isn't necessarily a bad thing! Going beyond your comfort zone can push you to grow as a person. You build skills when you attempt new things or get to know new people. Those skills make it easier for you to tackle a situation the next time you encounter it. Knowing and mastering new things helps build your self-esteem, improves your self-efficacy, and helps you engage in self-discovery. Self-esteem is how you evaluate your worth as a person, whereas self-efficacy is the belief that you are capable in a variety of contexts.[4] Self-discovery, in part, is the ability to have an accurate knowledge of your abilities and the effort to put those abilities into action.[5]

However, when you feel your boundaries or rights are being violated, that is a feeling of being emotionally or physically unsafe. Uncomfortable and unsafe are different.

There is also a difference between doing something out of fear or anxiety and exercising reasonable caution in the face of a real problem. Remember, as we discussed in the previous chapter, anxiety usually freezes you and prevents you from taking action. When you are having an anxiety attack, you can feel paralyzed. Your adrenaline is pumping and it's hard to think of what to do with your worries. When you are using reasonable caution, you are usually moved to *do* something. You can come up with options to help solve the problem, and then decide which course of action to take.

Bottom line: Trust yourself. If something doesn't feel right, it probably isn't. It is better to end a date or interaction and run the risk of looking "rude" than go along with things when you are feeling unsafe. If you want to talk to her later about how you were feeling, a reasonable person will be willing to have that conversation with you. If she isn't willing to talk about it, that's probably a sign that you made the right decision in leaving. You have the right to leave a situation at any time without feeling guilt or shame—that's a healthy boundary.

How to Set Boundaries When You Can't Block Contact

As we saw in Chapter 1, blocking contact is often the best option after you leave a toxic relationship or situation. However, sometimes you just will not be able to cut off communication, like when you have children together, will see each other at family events, or still work for the same company. There are ways you can protect yourself by establishing healthy boundaries.

Setting and Maintaining Boundaries with a Toxic Coparent

Setting boundaries with a toxic coparent is especially important because it's not just your safety and well-being on the line—your boundaries also protect your kids. In Chapter 1, I outlined some steps you can take to set boundaries with your ex, such as using an app to communicate and setting up a coparenting plan. Because coparenting may mean that a toxic ex-partner will stay a part of your life for years, let's go a little further and consider how you can maintain those boundaries for the long term.

Work with a Trusted Family Law Attorney

In Chapter 1, I recommended that you hire an experienced family law attorney to protect your interests as you work out the details of coparenting. A family attorney is an advocate for your legal rights and the rights of your children. A good attorney provides you with information to help you make the best decision for you and your kids while also letting you know the limits and potential drawbacks. An attorney will also let you know what she recommends as a course of action. How often you need to meet with your attorney depends on your situation, the adversarial nature of your coparent, and the number of issues you need to resolve. When you first meet with an attorney, give them an overview of why you are seeking their representation. Write down your questions ahead of time, and bring a document with the names, contact information, and location and date of birth for you and your coparent.

Also provide documentation of your finances, including shared and separate accounts for both you and your coparent. Also let your attorney know

- The ages of the children you share with your coparent
- Whether you have children with special needs that may need additional care
- Your priorities, including time-sharing, spousal support, staying in the marital home, or wanting to move out of state
- How long you have been married, and your date of separation (if applicable)
- What you are seeking as a resolution, including the amount of time-sharing you would like
- Your financial situation, including if you are paying for a majority of your children's expenses, and whether the coparent is refusing to contribute financially
- The assets you and the coparent share together, including vehicles, houses, or a shared business
- Who is currently living in the marital home, and whether you have discussed with your coparent if the house will be sold
- Whether the coparent has had any abusive behavior toward you or your children, including harassment and stalking

The attorney will ask you if they need any additional information. You may speak with a few attorneys to decide which is the best fit for you. Questions you may want to ask the attorney include

- What is your retainer (amount you pay up front) and hourly fee?
- How many cases have you worked on like mine?
- What is your preferred method of contact, and when can I expect a response?
- Who else would be working on my case?

- What are the possible outcomes for my case?
- Do you foresee any big issues?
- What is your approach to cases like mine?
- Am I being reasonable with what I want as an outcome?

Hire a Parent Coordinator

In many states, parent coordinators are licensed mental health professionals who have received special training and certification in high-conflict coparenting. Judges can appoint a parent coordinator in high-conflict coparenting cases, or you can hire one privately.

Your parent coordinator can walk you through creating a strong coparenting plan (more on that in Chapter 1 and in the next paragraph). You can also have ongoing discussions about other coparenting issues via the coordinator. For example, you may have a child that will be involved in baseball for the foreseeable future. How will you handle costs of his games, who will attend the games, and how will you handle the logistics and costs of out-of-town travel? Who will pay for any additional training if they seem to have promise as a ballplayer? You may have an elderly parent that will eventually move into your home, and your coparent may have an issue with your parent having contact with your children. How long you work with the parenting coordinator depends on the ability of both parents to work together, the number of children you have together, and the number of issues to be resolved. Sometimes, coparents find that working with a parent coordinator to resolve major issues is enough; some have continuing meetings with the parent coordinator.

Have a Detailed Parenting Plan

In Chapter 1, I recommended writing a detailed parenting plan that you and your ex agree on. The more detailed a parenting plan is, the less likely it will be that the high-conflict coparent will try to get around it. He may still try to push the boundaries, but you can fall back on the parenting plan as the "default" for your coparenting relationship. Hold to your established boundaries around time-sharing, exchanging the kids, and communication.

You may need to revisit the parenting plan as your kids get older. This is especially true if you want your child to go to a particular school, there is expected medical treatment as your child grows, or when your child will now be able to drive. For example, you may want your child to go to a specific high school, but right now they are ten years old. You may want to revisit the parenting plan around the time when your child may need braces to determine who will pay those costs and to agree upon an orthodontist. You may also want to revisit the parenting plan when your child is a teenager to determine whether a vehicle will be provided, which parent will provide it, and which parent will pay for insurance. You can write in your parenting plan that you will revisit the plan upon these events or when your child reaches a certain age.

You can also contact your attorney about changing the parenting plan if you are moving or if there has been a change in your availability and you would like to increase time-sharing. For example, you may have had a job where you were traveling half of the month, but you are now working locally and would like your child to be at your home more often. You may be moving closer to your child's school and would like to do more pickups and drop-offs. If you changed jobs and you have significantly less income, speak with your attorney if you need a modification of child support.

When a Child Gets in the Middle

It would be wonderful if children were not involved in any parental conflict—however, a toxic coparent may involve your child in your disputes. You may find that you are experiencing parental alienation. This is when a coparent tries to drive a wedge between you and your child, and is considered by many to be a form of child abuse.[6] Ways a toxic person may practice parental alienation include

- Having your child refer to you by your first name, and your ex-partner as "Mom" or "Dad"
- Leaving documents about the divorce or parenting plan in open view of the child

- Making disparaging comments about the coparent in front of the child
- Making comments to the child about having a lack of money due to the coparent
- Making unfounded accusations of abuse against the other parent
- Coaching the child to make statements against the other parent
- "Gatekeeping" or preventing the coparent from having her designated time with the child
- Talking to the child about reasons for the divorce or separation, including telling the child that the coparent had an affair
- Threatening to withhold affection or communication from the child if they don't align against the other parent

Remember not to sink to your toxic coparent's level, no matter how tempting it may be, or how much she tries to bait you into reacting. Anything you say or do may be used against you by the coparent or brought up in court. Keep documentation of any incidents where your child has been dragged into matters that should just be handled between you and your coparent, and report this information to your attorney.

Therapy may help your child cope with this difficult situation. Play therapists are specially trained in helping children express their feelings through play, as verbalizing issues can be difficult, even for adults. Pay attention to what your parenting plan says about having your child go to a therapist; it may say that you need approval from the other parent, or that the two of you must agree on the provider.

Establishing Boundaries in the Workplace

Some boundaries in the workplace are already enforced by federal and state laws, such as your right not to be discriminated against or harassed. However, there are many other ways that your boundaries can be put to the test.

You may see toxic people with the following behaviors in your workplace:

- Sabotaging your work by purposefully giving you the wrong instructions or taking credit for your work
- Refusal to take responsibility for their behavior
- Lack of empathy, especially in regard to how their behavior impacts others
- Lack of flexibility in solving problems
- Choosing a person or people to bully or harass
- Anger control issues
- Never satisfied with people, processes, or outcomes

If you feel you may be the target of someone's toxic behavior at work, first, look at whether the person behaved this way out of ignorance or malice. When a person acts out of ignorance, it is still a boundary violation, but the intent was not to hurt you. When someone acts out of malice, his goal *was* to hurt you. You may want to take a different approach for each of these situations. Maintaining healthy boundaries at work can be tricky, especially if you feel that someone may retaliate against you or there may be other ramifications. However, for your own well-being, it's crucial that you stand up for yourself, calmly and professionally:

- State your boundaries clearly and calmly to the person in question.
- Keep writing down any issues, including the date, time, and direct quotes.
- Review your employer's guidelines for reporting bullying and harassment.
- Consult with an attorney that specializes in workplace issues.

It may be difficult to know when an issue at work is solvable, and when it is most likely to continue and your best course of action is to leave. You may find it helpful to write out the pros versus cons of staying at that job. How much power do you have to create a change in your circumstances? Do the healthy relationships you've formed at work outweigh the toxic one? Is the job market such that it could be detrimental to your career if you leave?

Some coworkers or employers are so toxic that it isn't likely that their behavior will change. Sometimes, transferring to another department or floor is an option instead of quitting your job. Your employer may also be willing to have a hybrid work model where you work from home for part of the week. Brainstorm the options you have and be clear about your desired outcome. If you want to have a stress-free work environment, that may not be possible. However, being able to look forward to your day again may be an achievable goal.

If your quality of life is impacted to the point where you are losing sleep, undereating or overeating, having bouts of anxiety and depression, snapping at your loved ones, dreading waking up in the morning, or feeling suicidal, it may be time to leave. If you are suicidal, please contact the National Suicide Prevention Lifeline at suicidepreventionlifeline.org or 1-800-273-8255.

Establishing Boundaries with Family and Friends

If you have mutual friends with or are related to someone toxic, it can be tricky to enforce your boundaries even if you, yourself, aren't maintaining a close relationship with that person. You might still run into him or her at social occasions or on holidays.

If that person crosses a line with you, state your boundary calmly and with intention. It is best if this is done without an "audience" of others present unless you feel you need a witness. You aren't obligated to state why that boundary exists—you have a right to establish any boundary you want. You may need to use the "broken record" technique to restate your boundary repeatedly if the person appears to be ignoring your request or talking over you. Be willing to walk away from the conversation or person if your boundary is not respected.

If you are attending a family gathering where you may see a toxic relative, consider setting a time limit on your attendance, and have a healthy friend or family member act as a "buffer" for you. If the toxic person tries to approach you, your buffer can distract her.

If you are being sent messages from others who know the toxic person (see "No Flying Monkeys" on page 27), set clear boundaries that this person is not to be a topic of conversation. If the person persists in carrying a message or bringing up the toxic person, consider calmly stating, "I said this topic is off-limits," and walk away.

Boundaries are important in any relationship, not just a toxic one. As you are thinking about your boundaries, consider if your needs are being met in your other relationships. For example, if you have an otherwise healthy friendship with someone but notice that you are starting to do more "work" in the friendship, consider having a chat. Sometimes, just addressing concerns, as awkward as it might feel, can make a big difference in your relationships.

• • • • •

Boundaries are guidelines or limits you place on your behavior and the behaviors of others when they interact with you. In this chapter, you learned about the importance of establishing and maintaining healthy boundaries, whether it is in a romantic relationship, in the workplace, or with family and friends. Remember, you have a right to have boundaries and are not obligated to explain them to anyone. If you're having trouble with establishing or maintaining healthy boundaries, a mental health professional can help support you—and we'll discuss how to find that person in the next chapter.

6

TALK TO A PROFESSIONAL

How to Find and Work with a Mental Health Care Provider

S HARON WAS IN A QUANDARY. SHE AND HER HUSBAND, GARY, HAD BEEN married for ten years; her son, Ryan, had been in high school at the time. Ryan's dad wasn't very involved in his son's life, and Gary was a hands-on stepdad—most of the time, they got along well. But there had been some incidents when Ryan yelled and swore at Gary, and they knew that their son binge-drank at parties on the weekend. On Ryan's eighteenth birthday, he exploded at his stepfather and slammed out of the house.

Sharon always felt guilty after Ryan's outbursts—like maybe it was her fault that her son had anger issues. "Just give him some time to adjust," she pleaded.

"He's had three years," Gary said, adding that he felt Sharon was *enabling* Ryan's behavior by not enforcing their rules.

Ryan moved out when he went to college, and as the years went on, those teenage outbursts seemed like ancient history. Although his drinking had caused issues, he'd recently completed a treatment program. Sharon and Gary saw a bright future ahead, planning trips, saving for retirement, and looking forward to sharing holidays as a family. But then

Ryan was laid off from his job and called his mother to say he wanted to move back home.

Ryan arrived the following week. Sharon didn't tell Gary ahead of time because she didn't want to upset him. Of course, Gary got upset anyway when he realized that his stepson wasn't just there for a visit. He couldn't believe that Sharon hadn't even consulted with him about it.

The couple agreed that this would be temporary while their son looked for a new job, six months at most, and in exchange for room and board, Ryan would help with chores and stay sober. But, one year later, Ryan was still at home and unemployed. Sharon and Gary had been getting into arguments about Ryan not contributing to the household chores or looking diligently for work. He had also come home drunk a couple of times. Sharon was relieved Gary hadn't seen it and chose not to tell him about it to keep the peace.

The breaking point was when Ryan asked to borrow $5,000, after Gary and Sharon had already been taking money out of their retirement savings to help pay for their increased household expenses. "It's time for him to find another place to live," Gary said. "He needs to stand on his own!"

Sharon was torn. "I don't know what to do," she tearfully confided to her friend Tina. "I feel like I owe it to Ryan to help him however I can, after the divorce and his dad being so distant. But Gary—he's just reached his limit."

Her friend nodded sympathetically. "Have you thought about talking to somebody? A professional, I mean—like a therapist?" Tina asked.

Offended, Sharon asked, "What do you mean? I'm not *crazy!*"

"You don't have to be crazy to go to therapy," Tina said. "Everyone needs someone to talk to now and then. I did last year." Sharon hadn't even known her friend was going through something. "Here, let me give you my counselor's info. Or you can find somebody else. But I just really think talking to a counselor could help."

• • • • •

As I've mentioned often throughout this book, one of the essential steps toward healing is to get help from a professional trained in mental health issues. Now's the time to explore that step in detail.

You may be working with a mental health professional (MHP) already or have seen one in the past. If you can find one, it may be especially beneficial (and rewarding!) for you to talk to an MHP who specializes in helping people recover from narcissistic abuse and domestic violence and has experience with interpersonal relationship issues. In this chapter, you'll learn more about MHPs, how to know whether you've found a good fit with a helping professional, and the types of counseling they can provide.

I hope that you can find a professional you click with and have many productive sessions with him or her! That said, at the end of this chapter, I'll also cover how to know when it is time to decrease the frequency of your visits. But, before we get to all that, let's pause briefly and check in.

Your Pain Is Valid

Are you hesitating to take this step to start working with a mental health professional? If you're already working with one, are you holding back from discussing the toxic relationship with him or her?

If so, please know that you're not alone. Sometimes, people feel that what they are going through is not as bad as "other people have it." In subtle and not-so-subtle ways, people are told that they don't have a right to feel upset after an event because "others have it worse" and "you chose this." Toxic people especially may tell you that you have nothing to complain about. They are trying to invalidate how you feel and even prevent you from seeking help. If you don't seek help, then the ugly truth about the toxic person's behavior can still be a secret. Toxic people hate being exposed, as many are invested in their public image.

Your pain and trauma are valid, just as much as anyone else's experiences. You may feel that others have suffered through worse and that their pain is more "worthy" of treatment. Feeling this way may be a sign of the abuse you experienced from a toxic person. You may have experienced a pattern of being told you were "less than" or that you had nothing to complain about.

You may have been told that you should "just be grateful for what you have" rather than take care of your issues by talking with a professional. You have a right to your feelings, regardless of how many "good" things are happening in your life.

The process of therapy or counseling may seem awkward or uncomfortable at first. Sometimes, people have seen therapy sessions dramatized on shows or movies, and they are terrified of being "picked apart." You may not be sure about what happens in therapy sessions, or, like Sharon, you may have grown up with the message that only "crazy people" go to therapy. Please know that therapy is a normal process where you are bouncing ideas off a trained professional. We could all use a neutral person to talk to about what we've been through, what we're doing, where we're headed, and where we'd like to go. Think of therapy as kind of like having coffee with someone who happens to have training in human behavior. One of the nice things about therapy is that you can attend as little or as much as you want. You could even try it out a couple times and not go back, and that is okay (though if your first experience doesn't work out, I do hope you'll give it another try).

> "It really bothers me when someone says 'oh, first world problems' when someone talks about their suffering. We all have our issues to deal with, and one person's pain is just as valid as another's—we just have different pain."
>
> —Nour, 35

Who Are Mental Health Professionals?

MHPs—counselors, psychologists, social workers, and others—are trained to help you work through grief and rebuild your life. I'll use those professional titles more or less interchangeably throughout this chapter. A good therapist views your challenges for what they are—important, unique to you, and worth taking seriously. You have been through a lot in this relationship. You may feel that the people you usually rely on, while supportive, are having difficulty truly understanding what you are going through. Trusted friends and family are generally on your side and may not give you the objective support you need. An MHP is a neutral third party that can help you see what options are available to you, especially when you feel "stuck" after the breakup of a toxic relationship. MHPs can help you establish healthy boundaries and teach you how to enforce them, especially when you are around toxic people. Your therapist can help you validate your experiences and help you discover healthy self-soothing strategies. What's more, she can help support you as you work through the steps to healing in this book. That's why I strongly recommend you enlist the help of an MHP—of whatever type will best fit your unique situation.

MHPs include

- Psychiatrists
- Psychiatric nurse practitioners
- Psychologists
- Licensed mental health counselors/licensed professional counselors (LMHC/LPC)
- Social workers
- Marriage and family therapists

Each of these MHPs may help you; they just differ in training and years of experience. Psychiatrists and psychiatric nurse practitioners prescribe medication, and in a few US states, psychologists can prescribe medication as well. Psychologists, LMHCs, social workers, and marriage and family therapists can provide therapy and some also provide testing and assessment services. Whereas psychologists, LMHCs, and social workers can see people for individual therapy, couples therapy, and family therapy, marriage and family therapists have received special training in working with couples and families (and they can see people for individual therapy too). If you are seeing a therapist as a couple, it is usually recommended that you see someone else for individual therapy—and, as I noted earlier, a toxic partner may also try to manipulate a therapist. Many therapists will not see the same client for both individual and couples therapy, unless couples therapy is terminated.

"I see my counselor for talk therapy, and I see a psychiatrist for medication for my anxiety. I call them my 'mental health team.'"

—Gemma, 35

The most important thing is to find an MHP that is a good fit for *you*. You may need to meet with a few therapists to find the right fit. Sometimes, we "click" with people, and sometimes we don't. It's no different when finding a counselor. Get referrals from trusted friends, family, or clergy. Or do an online search for therapists in your area that specialize in narcissistic abuse and domestic violence.

CHECK-IN: IS THIS THE RIGHT THERAPIST FOR YOU?

When you first talk with a therapist on the phone or after your first session, review the following statements. Do you agree with the following statements?

1. I feel that I can speak to the therapist freely and without judgment.
2. I feel comfortable talking with the therapist.
3. The therapist seems personable and friendly.
4. I feel that this therapist listens to me.
5. The therapist answers the questions I have or is open about not knowing the answer to my questions.
6. The therapist is a licensed MHP and responds appropriately when I ask for a referral or about her license and certifications.
7. The therapist has experience working with survivors of abuse.
8. The therapist responds to emails and calls within 24 hours.
9. The therapist and I share a similar sense of humor.
10. The therapist let me know at our first session about confidentiality and my rights in counseling.
11. The therapist is knowledgeable and sensitive about my specific needs pertaining to my culture, gender, sexual orientation, religion/spirituality, and worldview.
12. This therapist challenges me in healthy and encouraging ways.

The more statements you agree with, the better the fit between you and the therapist. If you find that you didn't relate to these statements, reach out to someone else and keep looking for that better fit. If you've already started to work with that therapist and are coming to realize it's not working out as you'd like, see the section on discontinuing therapy (page 118).

A Word About Coaches

You may have seen advertisements or people on social media claiming they are "relationship coaches" or "life coaches." Be aware that coaching is not a regulated or licensed profession in any state or province. Whereas some MHPs are coaches, not all coaches are MHPs. So, make sure that the person you are working with is a licensed MHP.

A licensed professional has at least two years of rigorous graduate training, many hours of practicums and internships, and additional hours after graduate school to even qualify for licensure. Licensed MHPs not only have state and federal laws they need to follow—but they also all have a code of ethics. MHPs are held accountable by their state licensing boards, their certification boards, and their professional code of ethics. For example, a licensed mental health professional (called a licensed professional counselor in some states) needs to follow their state's laws and rules, the code of ethics and requirements of the National Board of Certified Counselors, and the code of ethics of the American Mental Health Counselors Association and the American Counseling Association. Many MHPs have also received additional training in specific therapeutic treatments, and some have achieved the highest status in their profession—being named a diplomate in their field. This is achieved after a clinician has shown substantial contributions to her profession. Ask to see an MHP's state license and credentials. You can also look her up online. Many states require an MHP to display her license in her office. If the person you are speaking with gives you any attitude about asking

"I asked a coach for proof of her credentials and she told me that she didn't have to show me anything. Next!"

—Jane, 22

for proof of licensure, he or she is not the right person for you. Legitimate MHPs will happily provide proof of licensure and credentials.

Types of Therapy

Therapy can come in different forms—individual, couples, family, or group.

Individual therapy (sometimes called talk therapy or psychotherapy) is when you see a therapist one-on-one. It's an opportunity to grow and receive support for challenging times in life.

In *couples therapy*, you and your partner work with the same therapist together. The counselor might be a licensed marriage and family therapist (LMFT) or another MHP with additional training in couples' issues. The therapist helps the couple resolve conflict and gain insight into their relationship dynamics.

Family therapy is often short-term. It gives family members a safe space to discuss issues. All family members might go, or just those who are willing to participate. The therapist will help the family develop skills to deepen connections.

Group therapy involves a counselor leading between five and fifteen people. Most are designed to bring together people dealing with a specific shared issue, such as coping with loss, overcoming substance abuse, or managing chronic pain, just as a few examples. Sharing your struggles with strangers may be intimidating at first, but it can offer a support network of people who can offer suggestions and hold you accountable.

After looking into these different types of therapy, Sharon decided that individual therapy was probably her best bet and made an appointment. At first, she didn't feel ready to tell her therapist, Ann, everything that she had been dealing with. But over her next few sessions, Sharon felt more comfortable sharing what was going on at home. She asked the counselor what she should do.

"I can't make that decision for you, but I can certainly help you explore all the options. Tell me more about Ryan," Ann said.

Sharon took a deep breath and told the story. After she finished, Ann said directly, "So, your son has been living in your home six months past when he was supposed to move out, he hasn't maintained sobriety, isn't helping out at home, isn't looking for work, has been disrespectful to Gary, and now is asking you for a large sum of money when you have already been paying some of his living expenses out of your retirement income." When the therapist summarized it in her own words, Sharon knew what she had to do.

When she got home, she sat down with Gary and Ryan. She told Ryan that he needed to find another place to live within two weeks, they would no longer be funding his lifestyle, and he needed to get sober. Sharon expected Ryan to go into one of his rages. Instead, he calmly said, "Okay," and walked off. He moved out one week later.

From that point on, Sharon's work with Ann shifted. She no longer needed to work through the immediate relationship challenges with Ryan, but she discovered she had a lot of pain and guilt to let go of related to her divorce. Sharon and Gary also started going to couples therapy to help repair some of the issues that had come to the surface when Ryan moved back home. Sharon felt she understood herself a bit better and would be better equipped to handle issues with the family in the future.

Therapeutic Orientations

Therapists have different types of training as well as what are called theoretical orientations, or "lenses," through which they see client issues. Four therapeutic orientations are very common—*cognitive-behavioral therapy* (CBT), *dialectical behavior therapy* (DBT), *solution-focused therapy*, and *acceptance and commitment therapy* (ACT). Most therapists have an eclectic style that combines different orientations.

If you have previously attended therapy and found that a particular orientation worked well for you, you may find it helpful to continue with a therapist that practices that same style. If not, you may want to try working with an MHP who uses a different approach.

Cognitive-Behavioral Therapy

Epictetus, a Greek philosopher, wrote, "People are not disturbed by things, but by the views they take of them." CBT has three core concepts about how you think and how it impacts the world around you. First, it's not an event that makes you upset or angry; it's the way you think about it that makes the difference. Second, you can become aware of and change your "inner dialogue." Third, a change in your thinking and inner dialogue can change how you see things and ultimately change your behavior.

In CBT, your therapist may talk with you about "thinking distortions" or ways of thinking that work against you. Sometimes, our inner dialogue is not very kind to us and can tell us things about events and ourselves that aren't true. Various types of thinking distortions include the following:

Magnification and minimization. Magnification is kind of like the saying "making a mountain out of a molehill." It means you are disproportionally upset about something that, in reality, is relatively small. An example would be thinking that you will get fired for showing up to work late simply because you can't find your car keys. Minimization is the opposite. It is taking a big event and making it seem like it is small and unimportant. An example is classic addictive behavior, where you tell yourself or others that the fact that you got wasted the night before is "no big deal."

Overgeneralization. Overgeneralization happens when thoughts about a one-time event are applied to all events in the future. An example would be if your friend says she can't go to lunch with you today and your inner dialogue responds, "I have no friends."

Personalization. Personalization happens when you think that events or other people's actions are a reflection of you. Very rarely in life are things personal—even when it feels deeply personal. How someone treats you is about them, not

"Through CBT, I realized that what people did and said to me was not a personal attack, and their behavior said more about who they were than anything about me."

—Jamal, 28

you. An example of personalization would be a friend sounding angry with you on the phone, so you wonder what you have done to upset them. In reality, your friend was just having a bad day.

Dialectical Behavior Therapy

DBT is a type of CBT. The goals of DBT include improving a person's stress tolerance, keeping emotions in check, and finding a balance between acceptance and change. One of the tenets of DBT is that it is perfectly normal to have competing emotions. You can simultaneously feel anger and attachment toward a toxic person. It may feel confusing, as many people are taught that we feel one emotion at a time.

In DBT, the acronym ACCEPT is used as a way to help you cope with stressors in your life.

A = Activities—Get active and do simple tasks to distract yourself from an upsetting event.

C = Contribute—Help out others in order to put your focus outside the self. For more information on the healing power of altruism, see Chapter 10.

C = Comparisons—Look at how your life is different from those who have a lot less than you do. Again, focusing outside yourself helps you deal with upsetting events. A gratitude journal, where you write down everything you are thankful for and what is going right, is a way for you to focus on all the good in your life instead of focusing on the upsetting parts.

E = Emotions—Act the opposite of whatever emotion you are having. If you are feeling tired, get active. If you are feeling sad, watch a funny movie. This practice shows you that emotions are temporary, and you have the power to change them.

P = Push away—Keep negative feelings at bay by visualizing yourself feeling competent and having influence over your own life.

T = Thoughts—Focus more on the logical part of your thinking. Emotions aren't facts. Look at what is true about your situation rather than focusing on speculation. Focus on what has happened rather than what you think happened.

Solution-Focused Therapy

In solution-focused therapy, your therapist may ask you what is going well right now or when you feel a decrease in stress, anxiety, or depression. Your therapist may also ask you, "How would things be if they were well?" In solution-focused therapy, this is known as the "magic question." It is a way to establish goals for your treatment and provide you with hope. A solution-focused therapist helps you define your strengths and methods to direct your energy to heal yourself. When you have been in a toxic relationship, you may feel that you can't do anything right or that you will never be in a healthy relationship. In solution-focused therapy, you find ways that you have already shown that you are strong and capable and have been able to form healthy relationships in the past.

One of the key concepts in solution-focused therapy is that when you change just one thing in your life, a cascade of positive benefits can result. For example, you have difficulty getting out of bed in the morning because life seems overwhelming, and you don't know whether you can face the day. You will lie in bed for an hour or two before you get up, and that's only because you have to use the bathroom. Your therapist might tell you that as soon as you wake up, you should sit up. Nothing else needs to change right now—just sit up. When you start sitting up first thing in the morning, you find it easier to get out of bed and start your day.

"I really appreciated my therapist asking what was going well in my life. I don't think anyone had asked me that before."

—Liesl, 45

Acceptance and Commitment Therapy

ACT focuses on experiencing your feelings rather than ignoring them or finding a distraction from them. It's normal behavior to avoid unpleasant emotions. However, when you don't deal with them, they pop up again, and sometimes in a more intense way. In ACT, you observe your feelings, experience them, and then let them go. You also work on forming your core values and learn how to navigate the world with those values in mind. Part of ACT focuses on mindfulness, the ability to stay in the present moment. (We'll revisit the concept of mindfulness in Chapter 7.)

Decreasing your emotional connection to your thoughts through a concept called *cognitive defusion* is a core principle of ACT. Cognitive defusion shows you that your thoughts don't change who you are, nor do you have to believe them. You can entertain a thought and dismiss it as not being true. One step of this process is to identify a negative thought, such as that you don't have value as a person. When you label this as just a negative thought, it loses its emotional power. You can also try repeating negative thoughts in a silly voice to distance yourself from them emotionally. You can also try "externalizing" the negative thoughts by saying, "Oh, that's just my brain doing its 'I don't wanna' routine." The more distance you place between your emotions and thoughts means greater acceptance and more room for healing.

I hope that one of these modalities appeals to you and gives you a starting point to look for a therapist whose style will suit you. If you wish to find out more, there are many resources that can tell you about different modes of therapy—check out the Resources section of this book.

Paying for Sessions

Once you've found a therapist you're interested in working with, the next question is how you'll cover the cost of sessions. It's true that therapy can be a substantial investment. But don't let the cost be an impediment to seeking help! You may have more options than you realize. You can pay for sessions out of pocket or with insurance. Additionally, your therapist may offer you a sliding scale of fees, or you may qualify for treatment at a reduced cost. There are also options you can explore if you have financial hardship; more on this follows.

Paying with Health Insurance

Let's cover insurance first. If you have medical insurance, check your summary of benefits and coverage to find out whether you have mental health benefits and what your insurance will cover. You can also give the insurance company a call and ask a representative. Make sure you get confirmation of your coverage in writing from the representative. You may have difficulties getting your insurance to honor a verbal statement from a representative. You will also need to confirm that your therapist accepts your particular insurance.

Even with health insurance, it's typical that your plan will cover only a portion of your session fees. Ask how many sessions your insurance will cover and at what percentage, as well as, if you'll owe a co-pay, how much that will be. Also ask about your deductible, as you may need to meet a particular threshold before insurance will cover your visits.

Keep in mind that if you are filing with your insurance company, your claim information goes into a national clearinghouse called the Medical Information Bureau (MIB) (mib.com). The MIB says they exist to combat insurance fraud. Still, your history of claim information can change your chances of getting life, disability, and long-term insurance (and until the Affordable Care Act, medical insurance). You can request a copy of your file on MIB's website. Review your file to make sure all the information therein is correct. If it is not, your doctor's office can submit a correction to the MIB. If there was a coding error, for example, a diagnosis was off by a digit, it can change your chances of getting insurance in the future.

College Counseling Services

Many college campuses provide individual and group counseling at no additional charge to students. These counseling services are included in the cost of your tuition. Counselor education departments on campus may provide counseling services at no charge as part of the training required of their graduate students. What you discuss in your campus counseling appointments is confidential, meaning that information will not be shared with university staff or faculty, your parents (unless you are under eighteen), or anyone else unless you sign a release of information. Exceptions to confidentiality include if you are suicidal or homicidal—MHPs may have a legal and ethical obligation to have you involuntarily hospitalized, but they usually give you an option to voluntarily hospitalize yourself first. Your campus counseling records are not part of your academic or administrative record. At the beginning of counseling you should be given a consent form that details your rights as a student using on-campus counseling services.

Paying with an Employee Program or Spending Account

You may also be able to get services—for you and for your family—at no cost under your employer's employee assistance program (EAP). EAPs are especially common at larger organizations, though many smaller companies offer them as an employee perk. Your EAP may also offer you a referral or compile a list of potential MHPs for you.

Your company may also offer you a health reimbursement account (HSA) or flexible spending account (FSA). Many mental health services, including some forms of online therapy, can be paid out of your HSA or FSA.

Paying Based on Your Income

If you don't have insurance, consider going to a therapist that offers pro bono (at no charge) sessions or sliding-scale fees. Sliding-scale fees are based on your income or ability to pay. The therapist may ask for a current pay stub to determine the tier of payment for which you qualify.

Finding Other Benefits

Suppose you are current or past military personnel, have an immediate family member in the military, have been in a natural disaster, or are

"I was able to get therapy at no charge through an organization that provides therapy to people who have been affected by gun violence. I don't know if I would have been able to afford it otherwise."

—Brady, 32

a victim of gun violence. In that case, you may qualify for pro bono (no charge) counseling. See the Resources section at the end of the book for more information.

Confidentiality

Therapists are held to high ethical standards. One of those is ensuring client confidentiality. This means that what you say to a therapist stays between you and the therapist, with a few exceptions. Those exceptions include

- He is subpoenaed by a judge to testify or produce your file.
- You are suicidal or homicidal.
- You have signed a release allowing your therapist to talk with a specific person.

"My mother left a long, rambling message for my therapist. My therapist told me about the message, and she told me that she didn't respond at all to my mother, as she didn't have a release—and even if she did have one, she would have talked it over with me in depth first. We then talked about how my mother leaving a message was further evidence of her violating my boundaries."

—Rick, 58

Confidentiality means that if a family member or your former partner contacts the therapist and the therapist doesn't have a signed release from you, the therapist cannot speak with that person. He isn't even allowed to confirm that you are a client.

Some toxic people will take it upon themselves to contact someone's MHP, so it is recommended that you do not share with this person that you are attending therapy or share the name of your provider. The toxic person will almost always use that information against you. When you first attend therapy, let your therapist know that you are concerned about this person contacting him. Your therapist can talk with you about your concerns.

You Get Out of Therapy What You Put into It

So, you've found a therapist and figured out how you'll pay for sessions in a way that you can manage. It should be easy from here, right?

If you haven't worked with a therapist before, I want to be candid: Therapy can be hard work. You may leave a therapy session feeling drained and tired; sometimes you will wonder whether it's worth it. It's challenging talking about your issues and the toxic relationship you survived. But keep in mind, while it's good for you and your MHP to click and even to share a sense of humor, therapy isn't supposed to be fun. The amount of effort you put into it is usually equal to what you get out of it. There can be moments of levity during sessions, of course, but overall you may feel that you did some work during the hour. You may also have sessions where your rapport with the therapist feels lighter and where issues seem less problematic. It's entirely normal for the seriousness of what you and your therapist talk about to vary from session to session.

That said, if you are having concerns about your feelings after a session, bring it up with your therapist the next time you see him. Your therapist can answer questions about the process of therapy. If you're not happy with the answer you receive, it may be time to discontinue treatment with that therapist so you can move on to another MHP.

> "Sometimes after sessions, I felt like I needed to take a nap. My therapist said this was normal, and to make sure I practice some good self-care in the days after my appointment."
>
> —Sam, 38

JOURNAL PROMPT: WHAT WOULD YOU LIKE TO ADDRESS IN THERAPY?

When going to therapy, it can be helpful to have a list or narrative of the concerns you would like to talk about. Write down where you would like to see improvements in your life, no matter how impossible solutions might seem. Therapy is your time to talk about what you want to talk about. (At least, after the initial intake session, which is less client directed because the therapist is learning more about you.) Sometimes, talking about things out loud in therapy helps you come up with new solutions. If you've tried solving the issues yourself, also write down what you have tried—and state whether what you tried made the issue better or worse. Bring this list with you to the therapist, or if you are doing telehealth, your therapist may have a client portal where you can upload the list.

KIDS AND THERAPY

If you are seeking therapy and you have children who are also dealing with the fallout from a toxic situation, consider finding an MHP for them too. Many MHPs specialize in treatment for children and adolescents.

Discontinuing Therapy

Therapy is entirely voluntary. You can decide at any time that you no longer want treatment—and you don't even need a reason. Sometimes, people just don't "click" with their therapist. Other times, they feel as though they have worked through their issues sufficiently enough that they don't need additional help. That's what happened for Kealoha.

Kealoha started therapy when she realized that her anger was getting out of control—it had contributed to the end of two relationships. She had been going to therapy every week for a few months, then every other week for a month. In therapy, she discovered the roots of her anger; not only had she endured abuse from her father, but she felt powerless against the ongoing marginalization of indigenous people in her home state. Her therapist helped her come to terms with how her anger had impacted her relationships. They also discussed ways that Kealoha could become more active in advocating for the preservation of her culture. Over time, Kealoha found that she was able to identify when she was starting to feel angry and express it in healthier ways. She had less and less to talk about in sessions. She and her therapist reviewed her original goals for therapy, and it appeared that Kealoha was able to handle life's complexities to her satisfaction without needing much assistance from her MHP. They mutually agreed it was time to end sessions—but, her therapist told her, he would always be there if she needed to talk to him again in the future.

All therapists have had clients that discontinued therapy at some point. So, letting your therapist know that you don't feel you need to come in anymore is something that they have talked to clients about before. You don't need to worry about hurting their feelings or leaving them in the lurch without a client to see; many therapists have waiting lists of new people hoping to begin treatment.

If you are having concerns or issues with your counselor, talk to him about it. Good MHPs always like to know if you have questions. Let your therapist know if you would like a referral to speak to someone else or if you have any questions about therapy. While therapists are good listeners, they aren't mind readers—you need to let them know when you have concerns.

What are some ways to address this with your therapist? Try one of the following:

- "I think I don't need to come in anymore."
- "I'm not sure if I'm getting what I need from therapy."
- "I'm not sure we click."
- "I think I can handle things better now."
- "I think I need to switch to a therapist that specializes in _____."
- "I think I've done all the work I can do here."
- "I think I'm good for now and don't need to come in."

Good therapists will always respond to you with kindness and professionalism. A vast majority of the time, your therapist will appreciate that you were direct about your feelings. Therapists support *autonomy*—this means that clients have the freedom to exercise their own choices, including discontinuing treatment. The goal of therapy is to feel that you can handle life's complexities without needing your therapist's guidance. You can always check back in with your therapist if you need them in the future.

If your therapist responds otherwise, consider that you made the right choice in deciding to end sessions. A caveat is if you are ending therapy due to pressure from another person.

During treatment, your therapist may recommend another MHP for your treatment. It could be that he or she is referring you to a psychiatrist for a medication evaluation. Your therapist may also refer you or transfer your care to another therapist. Your therapist may feel that another MHP is better equipped to help you. This is not personal—MHP ethics state that if someone is better able to provide you with the care you need, the therapist must refer you.

CHECK-IN: IS IT TIME TO END SESSIONS WITH YOUR THERAPIST?

You may be considering ending treatment with your MHP. To gauge whether you're ready, read over the following list. With which statements do you identify?

1. I feel I've reached a "plateau" in therapy. I still need to do some work, but we aren't getting anywhere.
2. I feel that I can navigate through life without the assistance of my therapist.
3. I feel that I have achieved my goals in therapy.
4. I think there may be a personality clash with my therapist.
5. I think another therapist might have more training in helping people who have been in toxic relationships.
6. I fundamentally disagree with some of my therapist's views.
7. My therapist is habitually late or has not shown up for one of my appointments.
8. I think my therapist and I are just not the right fit for each other.
9. My therapist has violated one or more of my boundaries.

If you identified with *any* of these statements, it might be time to end your therapeutic relationship. If your therapist has violated boundaries, read the next section on what to do.

JOURNAL PROMPT: WHAT HAVE YOU LEARNED IN THERAPY?

If you are considering ending therapy or stepping down on your visits, it can be helpful to look back at all you have learned. What changes have you made in your life as a result of going to therapy? How have you changed as a person? Do you find that you are better able to handle the complexities of life? Write down all the ways you have benefited from therapy, including unexpected benefits, such as noticing that your relationship with your partner has improved.

What if There Has Been a Boundary Violation with Your Therapist?

Suppose you feel that something inappropriate has occurred with a therapist. First, as I said earlier, it may be a good idea to talk to them about it. If the issue is not resolved to your satisfaction, you can report the event to the therapist's licensure or certification board. You may be contacted by the board(s) to provide additional information. In the meantime, stop sessions with the therapist.

However, if you feel that discussing the issue with your therapist puts you in imminent danger or if the violation is severe, consider just reporting it instead of talking it over with them first.

Know that a vast majority of mental health professionals have only your best interests in mind. Unfortunately, just like in any professional field, a few should not be in the profession and can cause harm. And since clients are vulnerable and talking about personal issues, there is a potential for them to cause more damage. You do have avenues to seek resolution.

• • • • •

Talking to a neutral third party like a mental health professional can help you work through your feelings and the possible trauma you may have suffered during a toxic relationship. In this chapter, you learned about the process of therapy and what you might gain from it. Most important, you learned that your pain and experiences are valid, and you are worthy of expressing those feelings to someone who is trained in helping you.

A good MHP will also find self-soothing strategies and ways for you to take care of yourself when you aren't in the counseling office. This is all part of good self-care—and that's the topic of the next chapter.

7

PRACTICE SELF-CARE

How to Make Sure Your Needs Are Met and
Build Care into Your Daily Routine

A TOXIC PERSON MAY HAVE TOLD YOU—EITHER THROUGH WORDS OR actions—that your needs weren't important. When you're recovering from a toxic relationship or situation, now is the time to be extra good to yourself and, if you don't do it already, practice tender loving self-care.

Self-care isn't a luxury that you can add to your life sometimes. It is a necessity. It's common to believe that self-care is an indulgence or that we should put other people's needs before our own, but that couldn't be more untrue! When we practice self-care, we make sure we have the energy and calm mind that we need to really heal. This chapter clears up common misconceptions about self-care and explores some of the many ways to practice self-care.

> "My therapist told me that self-care, when you are a caregiver, is like when you are on an airplane, they tell you to put your oxygen mask on before your child's—you need to take good care of yourself first so you can take care of others."
>
> —Meghan, 35

What Is Self-Care?

Self-care doesn't mean being pampered or getting "special treatment." It is the act of treating yourself as well as you would treat your best friend. It is striving for health and wellness in various areas of your life, including your physical, emotional, spiritual, and social well-being. If you're wondering what wellness means in each of these areas, let's take a look.

Physical: Physical well-being is what most of us think of first when we consider the idea of "health." Self-care practices in the physical realm include attending regular doctor and dental appointments, getting consistent exercise, having good sleep habits, maintaining good hygiene, and eating a balanced diet.

Emotional: Emotional well-being is acknowledging your feelings and allowing yourself to feel them. When you experience a strong emotion, instead of feeling out of control, you know that feelings are part of the human experience. You know when you need to take time off to recalibrate when you are feeling stressed or run-down. You practice proactive instead of reactive self-care—meaning you take care of yourself on a consistent basis, not simply as a reaction to feeling stressed.

Spiritual: Spiritual well-being means that you feel connected to something larger than yourself. This doesn't necessarily mean that you subscribe to a religion—it means that you have a code of ethics or tenets that you live by and that inform your decisions. You may feel a connection to the environment and other living things. Practicing spiritual self-care could involve going to a place of worship, praying, meditating, or being in nature.

Social and family: Social and family wellness means that you feel connected to others, are active in your community, and maintain a balance among other areas of your life and the time you spend with your friends and family. You are able to say no to social engagements and responsibilities without feeling guilt. You are empathic toward others and set healthy boundaries. Practicing self-care here means knowing when you need social support and reaching out to others—as well as recognizing when you need time for yourself and taking it.

JOURNAL PROMPT: HOW IS YOUR WELLNESS?

For each of the wellness areas in the previous section, give yourself a rating from 1 to 10. A 1 indicates an area in which you need a lot of additional help. A 10 indicates that you are very satisfied with how that area of your life is going.

Choose one of the areas in which you feel you could use improvement. Then, brainstorm some ways to get there. For example, if you said your physical well-ness was a 2 and you would like it to be an 8, steps you could take include going for a walk every day, using a pill organizer so you are consistent with your medication, and going to bed at ten p.m. every night. If you think you can consistently do one or two of those things for a month, give it a shot. When you start to see the positive changes you are making, you are more likely to stick with those changes over the long term. But take it one step at a time—don't feel that you have to totally change your habits in every wellness area at once!

	CURRENT STATE 1–10	WHERE YOU'D LIKE TO BE	STEPS TO TAKE
Physical			
Emotional			
Spiritual			
Social			

After a month, return to this activity. How are you feeling in that area now? Ready to take on another? Do the same thing for another area where you want to make improvement. Over time you'll see big improvements in your overall quality of life.

Self-Care Isn't "One Size Fits All"

As you read this chapter, some self-care practices might appeal to you, and some others . . . not so much. That's completely fine! What works for one person might not work for you. Your friend may find a day working in her garden to be the ultimate way to unplug, while you'd rather stay inside and read. She might take a long bath to relax, but you just get bored and want to get out of the tub. It doesn't mean that you are doing self-care incorrectly—it just means that people have different ways to unwind. You may need to try out other techniques before you find a few that work. Think of a time when you were stressed out and then felt some relief. What were you doing at the time? Try re-creating that and see whether it works now to help you relax and recharge.

CHECK-IN: HOW AM I DOING WITH SELF-CARE?

An effective way to assess how you're doing with self-care is to check in with yourself. How many of these statements ring true for you?

1. I am meeting everyone else's needs before my own.
2. I feel that I don't make much of a difference.
3. I am doing the same things every day and feeling run-down.
4. I just don't have enough energy.
5. I wake up feeling tired, not refreshed.
6. I think about running away and starting over.
7. I find it hard to say no to others.
8. I usually don't take time out of my day to just enjoy life.
9. I am not very physically active.
10. I don't have a go-to relaxation technique.

The more statements you agreed with, the more you need to brush up on your self-care strategies. Again, take it one step at a time—try to find one self-care practice you can stick with to start.

Take Time for Fun

A toxic person may have told you that having fun was something you had to "earn," and you were constantly falling short of his impossibly high expectations. You deserve to be happy. You can have fun without anything terrible happening to you.

So, do something each day just for the sake of enjoying it. You can do whatever you want, given that it doesn't hurt you or someone else. You no longer need to hear from the toxic person that your hobbies and interests are "less than."

It may be helpful to get out of your home to fully enjoy yourself. When you are at home, you may start thinking about cleaning or chores. Getting outdoors can be a powerful way to shift your focus from tasks to just enjoying yourself. Nature tends to have a slower pace than daily life, so you may find yourself automatically slowing down your thoughts.

You can have fun on your own, or you can include friends and family. Make sure that they are entirely on board with having a relaxing time and agree to save challenging topics of conversation for another time. Otherwise, you may find yourself trying to soothe them instead of enjoying yourself!

When you are having fun, note what you are doing that gives you joy. Are you playing a game with your family? Are you cooking, gardening, or hanging out with friends? What are you doing when you forget about your stress and are enjoying the moment? It might feel silly, but I actually do recommend that you write those things down. When you need a break, take out that list of fun activities you created, and pick one.

Having fun doesn't necessarily cost you anything—there are many enjoyable activities you can do for free. Look up what is happening in your community for activities that are low to no cost.

> "It was hard for me to let loose and have fun because my ex-boyfriend always told me I never took our relationship seriously. I found out I could have fun without feeling guilt and shame."
>
> —Sarah, 50

Eat Well

Many of the self-care strategies in this chapter are helpful to everyone, but particularly so if you are coping with or have left a toxic relationship. Eating healthy is another one of those self-care strategies that should make anyone feel better, but it's especially important when you are experiencing loss and chronic high-level stress. Food is medicine and fuel for our body. While you are coping with the aftermath of a toxic relationship, you need the best medicine and fuel possible. Prioritize regular meals. Eat when you're hungry and stop when you feel full.

When we aren't feeling good, we tend to gravitate toward carbohydrates and sugary foods and can develop addictions to food.[1] Binge-eating or restricting your eating is also more likely to happen when you are under severe stress, especially if you have a history of an eating disorder. Please see your doctor or a mental health professional if you feel that you may be reverting back into eating-disordered behavior. It is a slippery slope back to relapse, so make sure you address it as soon as possible.

Consider meeting with a registered dietitian to discuss a healthy eating plan. If you enjoy cooking, find a new healthy recipe to try. Try eating mindfully (see page 133).

Maintain Your Physical Hygiene

We usually don't have difficulties with daily living skills unless we are experiencing depression, anxiety, trauma, extreme stress, or grief—all of which are common after leaving a toxic relationship or situation. We can forget to take care of basics, such as showering, changing clothes, sleeping, or eating. These things may sound very obvious, but when you're struggling, the simplest things can seem terribly hard. These small steps can help.

It can be very tempting to stay in bed when you aren't feeling good. But the simple act of getting out of bed can make a world of difference toward feeling better. As soon as you wake up in the morning, sit up and then get out of bed.

Next, change out of your pajamas into clean, comfortable clothing.

If you're having difficulty focusing on what you need to do in the morning, post a list of your morning and evening routines somewhere you'll see it, such as on your bathroom mirror.

If you find yourself skipping personal hygiene, consider meeting with a mental health professional (revisit the previous chapter for more info if you need it). It can be helpful to talk out your experiences with someone, and you may benefit from a medication evaluation as well.

Exercise

Movement is an essential part of staying healthy. If you haven't exercised regularly, it may seem daunting and uncomfortable to begin an exercise routine. However, once you start moving and see the benefits, such as reduced stress, increased energy, and less pain, it may become less like work and more like a fun way to take care of yourself.

Focus more on "movement" rather than "exercise"—and any type of movement counts. You may consider taking the stairs instead of the elevator at work or having a dance party with your kids.

Here are some other ways to get moving:

- Take a walk during your lunch break.
- Sit on a large exercise ball while you are at your desk or on the phone.
- Do household chores, especially deep cleaning.
- Ride your bike when you would usually drive.
- Do yard work.
- Engage in quick bursts of activity while watching a video, in between episodes or during commercials.
- Walk while you talk on the phone.
- Invite friends to an activity that requires movement, such as taking a dance class together.
- Invest in virtual reality and take walks all over the world, or use a VR fitness app.
- Dance it out to your favorite songs.
- Become a referee or coach for your favorite sport, or coach a kids' team.

To get the most benefit from a workout, do it first thing in the morning. You will receive more benefits from the dopamine and endorphin boost exercise gives, such as increased focus and relaxation. Exercising first thing in the morning also helps you cross it off your list—it may be more difficult to exercise after working all day.

When you get regular exercise, you not only reduce your stress but also boost your mood. You also feel a sense of mastery over the activity you are doing, which improves your feelings of self-efficacy.[2] Self-efficacy is the belief that you can succeed in doing something. Right now, it might be especially impactful for you to feel that you are making progress in learning something new and conquering it, especially if a toxic person told you repeatedly that you couldn't do anything on your own.

> "I didn't want to do anything labeled 'exercise.' But then I found out that walking on the beach with my friends counted as exercise. Now it's not such a big deal."
>
> —Sarah, 42

Keep a Journal

With all the prompts throughout this book, you've probably noticed that I am a big proponent of journaling. Journaling helps you process your emotions, and it also gives you a way to look back and see your personal growth, both emotionally and spiritually. Journaling helps your emotional and physical health. If you've been in a toxic relationship, you may have noticed flare-ups of existing health issues due to the level of chronic stress you have endured.

When you journal, you dump thoughts and feelings onto the page. Your brain thanks you for getting that stuff out and in the open. By externalizing your thoughts and feelings, your brain has less to carry around.

You may think that journaling means you write your thoughts down in a book. That's a classic, but there are many different ways to journal—this isn't a one-size-fits-all kind of self-care practice. Any level of writing skill is just fine for a personal journal. If you prefer to talk out loud about your ideas as a way to process them, or if you just don't like to write, consider dictating your thoughts or recording them. You could do something as simple as just speaking your thoughts into your phone for a few minutes while you sit in your car in the parking lot during your lunch break. A journal also doesn't have to consist of words—you can also create sketches and even paint.

There is also no "right" amount of time to journal. While there is evidence that the more you journal, the better you will feel, the fact that you are journaling at all is significant. Progress is progress.

Every so often, review your journals. You may want to do this process with a therapist's assistance, especially if you are a trauma survivor. As you look over what you wrote, keep focusing on how much you have grown as a person throughout your healing process. We tend not to notice changes as much when we are in the midst of them. But when we look back, we can see great moments of progress. We can also see times when we thought we wouldn't make it through something, yet here you are, beating the odds.

A few words of caution here: If you are still in contact with a toxic person, they may attempt to access your journal. You can keep a journal in a password-protected encrypted file on your device rather than in a paper version. However, someone with enough determination and skills can access anything on an electronic device. If you are currently in litigation over child custody or think that there is a chance you might be going to court in the future, contact your attorney about whether you should keep a journal. In some states, a journal that is part of your counselor's assigned treatment is not "discoverable" in legal terms, but journals kept for private use (not part of therapy) may be discoverable. Discoverable means that an opposing party may request to see your journal through a legal process.

> "Whenever I feel like I am being hoovered back into contact with my toxic friends, I look back over my journals and see how much better I have been feeling since I blocked them. It's a good reminder of how far I've come."
>
> —Javier, 26

JOURNAL PROMPT: WRITE HOW YOU ARE FEELING IN THIS MOMENT

If you're new to journaling or just would like to focus on the present moment, writing down how you are feeling right now can be a helpful practice. Describe *your mood in as much detail as possible. How are you feeling? If you are feeling sad, try to go deeper with your feeling. Are you feeling disappointed, miserable, troubled, heartbroken, dejected, pessimistic, or somber? If you are feeling happy, are you feeling elated, joyful, pleased, content, peaceful, delighted, ecstatic, or upbeat? Sometimes, people describe their mood with colors, compare it to places and experiences in their lives, and even compare their mood to animals. For example, a person might describe their anger "like a tiger, ready to pounce. It is an angry red. It is a feeling of injustice, of things not being fair." Drawing a picture of your mood might help you think of it in a different way.*

Make this a regular practice in your journaling. Notice how you are better able to process and let go of how you are feeling when you have written it out.

Meditate

Meditation is the practice of staying in the present moment. It can be as simple as focusing on your breathing—noticing your inhaling and exhaling. In some forms of meditation, you are sitting or lying down. Some people practice *mindfulness meditation*, where being active during meditation is not only welcome, it is encouraged.

Sometimes, when you are meditating, you may experience what's often called "monkey brain": many thoughts crossing through your mind, just as a monkey swings from branch to branch. It is perfectly normal to experience monkey brain. The goal of meditation is not to empty your mind—even people who have meditated for years will tell you that it is virtually impossible. The goal is to have more awareness of yourself and to stay in the present moment. When you are meditating, you may see a thought drift into your mind. Acknowledge the thought, and then let it go. The more you meditate, the more you may find it is easier to let your thoughts go when they enter your mind.

Some apps and recordings can guide you through meditation. See the Resources section for more information.

Mindfulness

Mindfulness is a type of meditation where you stay active while simply focusing on the present moment. Distractions are welcomed in mindfulness practice, as our lives tend to be busy.

One mindfulness practice you can try is eating mindfully. When you sit down for a meal, turn off any devices, including your television. Focus just on eating your food. As you eat, chew each piece of food at least ten times, focusing on the texture, taste, and smell. You may find that when you eat mindfully, you eat less food and still feel satisfied. You may also start gravitating toward eating healthier foods since you are now fully paying attention to eating.

Name Three Things

When you are feeling stressed or are triggered into having flashbacks to abuse, try the "name three things" technique. You don't even need to move to practice it—stay right where you are if you'd like. Name three things you can hear, three things you can see, and three things you can feel. Repeat naming three things until you feel that you are back to feeling like yourself. You can name the three things out loud or silently. You can name the same things each time or choose different things. This practice is known as a *grounding technique*. A grounding technique helps distract your brain and get it to focus on the present moment. The more you practice the "name three things" technique or another grounding technique, the easier it will be to remember it when you are stressed.

Try Creative Visualization and Guided Imagery

Take advantage of your brain's ability to be creative and use it to produce feelings of relaxation. There are many recordings and videos available online that walk you through a relaxing scene. Some will count you down into a relaxing setting and then count you back out when it is time to wake up or return to regular activities. Other recordings will count you down into a relaxing state and then let you sleep.

You may have to try different recordings before you find one that works for you. Some narrators' voices may be more appealing than others; some imagery may be more comforting to you than others.

Get Enough Sleep

Getting a good night's rest is one way our brain heals itself, and it makes coping with day-to-day life much easier. Practicing good sleep hygiene is a must in healing from toxic relationships. A toxic partner may have purposefully kept you up at night as a way to control and intimidate you. It might have been years since you have had a restful night of sleep.

There are several ways you can help yourself get a good night's rest, which is especially important if you are sleeping on your own for the first time in a while.

- Listen to a relaxing recording before bed.
- Turn off all electronic devices at least an hour before bed.
- Move your television out of the bedroom.
- Get a new mattress if yours is older or uncomfortable.
- Keep pets out of the bedroom.
- Use the bed only for sleeping and sex, not for work.
- Make your bed and bedroom a relaxing and comfortable place by reducing clutter and using soft lighting.

Talk to your doctor if you are having problems sleeping. Let her know if you have a family history of sleep issues. You may need medication to help you get to sleep, at least temporarily. Taking medication (as prescribed) to help you sleep can help you better control your mood and stress the next day. In turn, getting enough sleep enables you to heal and be more hopeful about rebuilding your life.

"I started turning off my phone and tablet an hour before bed, and I felt much more rested in the morning."

—Sade, 28

Use Electronic Devices in Moderation

As I mentioned in the previous section, it's generally recommended that you turn off electronic devices at least an hour before bed. Why? Your brain needs a chance to unwind. When you look at backlit devices before bed, the light they emit suppresses melatonin in your brain.[3] Melatonin is a hormone that helps regulate sleep. You may think that using the dimming or "nighttime" feature on your phone helps, but unfortunately, it doesn't improve melatonin suppression.[4] So, that means giving yourself a break from the computer, tablet, phone, or TV before bed. If you wake up in the middle of the night, don't turn them on.

Consider having a "no electronics after nine p.m." rule that applies to you and to other people in your home too. If a full hour is challenging, first try shutting them off fifteen minutes before bed. You may find that you feel more refreshed in the morning. Then work your way up to shutting electronics off thirty minutes before bed, then forty-five minutes, and then the full hour. Working your way toward a habit is called *shaping a behavior*, and it's a helpful way to ease into change.

Limit Social Media Use

Limit your interactions on social media for the time being. More and more, mental health professionals and others are realizing that social media comes with some serious drawbacks. The more time you spend on social media, the greater your chances of having symptoms of depression and anxiety.[5] There are a few reasons for this, and I'd like to highlight two.

First, when we see people's happy posts or photos, it's easy to start comparing our lives to theirs and wonder why ours seems to be much more difficult. As the saying goes, "comparison is the thief of joy." There will always be people who have more and less than we do. It's also important to remember that much of what people post is not an accurate reflection of their day-to-day lives. We never really know what goes on offline. You may have experienced that yourself in your toxic relationship—you and your former partner may have appeared to have it all, but your friends or followers on social media never knew what you were really going through.

Next, our sense of self-worth can get tied up with how many likes or positive comments we get on a post. Getting a thumbs-up or a heart on a post feels really good. It's just our brain chemistry—getting a like or comment on social media triggers a dopamine release in your brain, lighting up your internal "reward system."[6] This feels good for anyone, and especially for someone who just came out of a toxic situation where they might not have gotten much validation. Our brain gets used to this. And then, not getting as much feedback on a post can ruin your day. Remember, the amount of feedback you get on a post or video is not a reflection of your value as a person. You may know that logically, but your brain sends you other signals.

Social media also create distance that lets people make harsh comments that they'd never make in a face-to-face interaction.

If you find it difficult to avoid social media, you may have to uninstall apps from your phone or tablet or deactivate or delete your accounts. (It sounds drastic, but it's worth it to protect yourself—and you may find yourself enjoying the time you've now gotten back in your day!) If you have to be on social media for your job, consider shutting off comments if it is difficult for you to avoid them entirely. Engagement with followers does help, but consider the cost to you when you read negative comments.

"I would get really upset with myself, wondering why everyone was having such a great life while I was struggling with rebuilding my life. I saw all their photos of their happy relationships, babies, and exotic trips they were taking. Then I realized that all those people had struggles too—they just didn't post that stuff online."

—Constance, 40

If you are still using social media, make sure you block the people associated with your former partner. If blocking a person would stir up trouble or even reignite contact with toxic people, mute them instead. If there are posts that you find triggering or provoking, you can block posts that contain specific words, such as "abuse," "self-harm," and "narcissist."

Don't Trade One Addiction for Another

After the initial sense of relief you feel in ending an unhealthy relationship, a feeling of emptiness may arise. Even when you know you made the right decision, it still leaves a void of someone you used to spend time with, talk with, and be physically intimate with. That loss can feel overwhelming. Darby could tell you all about that.

Darby and his ex, Micah, split up after a year-long relationship that had started out promising but slowly became unhealthy. Things fell apart after Micah flew into yet another narcissistic rage. Darby realized that being single would be better than being in a partnership with someone who was out of control—so he left and went no contact. Although Darby had been in longer partnerships before, the grief was harder than after any other breakup he'd been through. In the six months since the breakup, Darby had gone on some dates, but no one really sparked his interest. He was living on his own, and he was really tired of thinking about Micah, wondering who Micah really was, and, worst of all, how he could still miss his ex after how he had behaved. Darby felt that just having one or two drinks would stop him from ruminating about it. But over time, Darby noticed that he had to drink a little more to avoid feeling lonely. He started staying home more, and dating seemed pointless—besides, what if the guy turned out to be just like Micah? One or two drinks a night was turning into four or five, and Darby had trouble contemplating a night without a bottle of wine.

After leaving a relationship with addictive tendencies (think of the push-pull phenomenon I described on page 83), many people replace one addictive behavior or process with another—seeking the high they once got from reconciliation with a toxic partner through something else instead. That addictive substance or activity might be alcohol, drugs, porn, food, or even overexercise; it's anything that is having a negative effect on your life that you find difficult to stop. Addiction serves two purposes. It soothes feelings of loss, anxiety, and depression, and it also relieves us from having to deal with things we would rather not face.

One day, Darby's friend Heather called him on it, commenting to him that he seemed to be drinking more than usual.

Darby got defensive. "You don't know what you're talking about, Heather," he said.

Heather shook her head. "Darby, my dad was an alcoholic. I can see the signs. I'm worried for you, and what might happen if you don't stop." Darby didn't talk to Heather for two weeks after that. But eventually he realized his friend confronted him because she cared. And he wasn't drinking just to avoid feeling bad about the breakup and being lonely—he was drinking so he didn't have to feel *anything*. He made an appointment with his doctor to talk to him about making changes.

Bottom line: Trading one addiction for another is common, but you have the power to identify it and get it under control. If you're feeling like you might be at risk of trading one addiction for another, try using some of this chapter's self-care strategies as healthier ways to soothe yourself. You might also benefit from working with a counselor. Let's check in.

CHECK-IN: HAVE YOU STARTED OR RESTARTED AN ADDICTIVE BEHAVIOR?

Think about an addictive substance or activity you might have used or engaged in recently. How many of the following statements do you identify with?

1. I am finding it difficult to control my use.
2. I have gotten in legal trouble due to my use.
3. Family and friends have expressed concern about my use.
4. I have tried to control my use, but it's not working.
5. I have gone into debt due to my use.
6. I have missed important events in my life due to my use.
7. I have prioritized my use over essential people in my life.
8. I can't see myself ever being free of using.
9. I have experienced withdrawal symptoms, such as cravings.
10. I am considering going back to the toxic person in my life to get more access to what I am using.

If you have answered yes to at least one of these statements, you may be experiencing addiction and dependency. If you find that you are leaning on a substance or behavior to get you through complicated feelings, talk to a mental health professional who has training in addictions. Revisit the previous chapter for more information on how you can find support.

Build In Time for Self-Care

You may feel that you don't have the time to practice self-care. I hope, after reading this chapter, you can prioritize self-care in the things you're probably doing anyway—sleeping enough, eating well, and maintaining your hygiene. To add in a few other daily self-care practices, such as journaling, meditation, or exercise, try the following:

- **Just take five.** Even practicing self-care for a few minutes at a time counts—it's better than nothing!
- **Break it into small blocks.** Think you don't have an hour to exercise? How about taking ten minutes now, and another few minutes later? It all adds up.
- **Schedule a self-care appointment.** You may need to schedule self-care time on your calendar and say no to other activities during that set time. When you set boundaries on your availability, people tend to be more respectful of your time.
- **Take a trip or self-care staycation.** If you have the resources, taking a self-care trip can help distance you from everyday distractions that you're prioritizing instead. If you can't travel, consider blocking off some of your days as a designated time for rest and healthy activities.
- **Make it a ritual.** If you designate the same time every day or every week to do the same practice, it becomes a habit. For instance, you might write or doodle in your journal every day at six p.m.

When you start practicing self-care and see how it improves your mood, perspective, and how you interact with the world around you, it positively reinforces that behavior—so you may be naturally drawn to build in more self-care time.

• • • • •

Taking good care of yourself is essential to your healing. In this chapter, we explored self-care strategies such as getting enough sleep, exercising, journaling, and taking time to check in with yourself through meditation. When you practice proactive self-care, you are keeping yourself healthy before a crisis hits. When you take care of yourself, you can better fulfill the other responsibilities in your life and be present and available for others. In the next chapter, we'll explore how reconnecting with healthy people in your life can help you rebuild.

8

RECONNECT

How to Rebuild Relationships with Emotionally Healthy People

JULES FELT SHE HAD A PRETTY SOLID SUPPORT SYSTEM—SHE GOT ALONG fairly well with her family, and she had some very close friends. But lately, Jules's friends had become busy with their kids, and she didn't see them as often as she would have liked. One day, Jules decided to sign up for a cooking class to meet people. She immediately hit it off with one of the other attendees, Sandy, who was new in town. The two later met for coffee, and it wasn't too long before they were hanging out every weekend. "I've never had a best friend," Sandy gushed, "but spending time with you just makes me feel whole."

"That's so sweet!" Jules exclaimed. "I've been missing spending time with friends, and I'm glad I met you too." Sandy must have taken that as a signal because she launched into many stories of past friendships that had gone sour. Seemed like she had a pattern of going out of her way to help friends only to have them take advantage of her and cut her out of their lives. Privately, Jules thought it was a little odd for the woman to be sharing so much so early, but, she reasoned, at least it was cool that Sandy felt comfortable sharing her past after being burned.

A few weeks later, Jules's friend Meghan called and wanted to catch up. Jules gladly agreed, adding, "And you have to meet my new friend,

Sandy!" Meghan got along well with everyone, Jules thought, so it would be good to introduce the two so Sandy would know someone else in town.

The three of them met at Jules and Sandy's new regular coffee shop. Sandy seemed to be shutting the other woman out of their conversation, at one point actually turning her chair so her back was facing Meghan. Later that night, Meghan called Jules. "I don't know how to put this," she began, "but there is something really off about your friend."

"I don't know," Jules replied. "She's probably nervous to meet someone new—she's been through a lot. Maybe you're being a little critical." The two hung up on a much frostier note than usual.

The next morning, Sandy called. "I just want to be a good friend," she said. "So, I feel obligated to tell you what Meghan said about you. She said you're clingy and too demanding of her time." Jules briefly wondered when the two had even spoken alone—but after last night's conversation, Sandy's revelation struck a nerve. Too angry to broach it with her old friend, she stopped talking to Meghan.

A few weeks later, Jules invited Sandy over for dinner with her family. Everything seemed to go well. But when Sandy went home, Jules's mom turned to her angrily. "I had no idea you were so ungrateful." Jules had no idea what her mother was talking about, but her mom wouldn't hear it.

After that, she and her mother started spending less time together. Over time, Jules was only socializing and talking with Sandy. Until one day at the coffee shop, when Jules came back from the restroom only to catch Sandy hurriedly shoving something into her purse. Later, Jules discovered cash was missing from her wallet. And her favorite earrings were gone from her dresser too. It was a major wake-up call for her—how could she have missed the red flags?

She distanced herself from Sandy and eventually cut off the friendship. But Jules felt utterly alone. The loss of her fun new "friend" left her noticing a major hole in her life. She longed to have her old connections with her family and friends back, but she felt guilty and ashamed for falling for Sandy's manipulation and separating herself from them. After all this time, she wasn't sure how to reconnect.

· · · · ·

When you were in a toxic relationship or situation, you may have become isolated from your friends and family. Like Sandy, a toxic person might have stirred up conflict between you and your other friends. You might have heard that someone thinks you're crazy or too dependent. These lies may have shaken your trust in other people. This is a common part of a toxic person's goal—to isolate you as much as possible and make you distrust people so you must depend on him or her.

As part of your healing process, reach out to friends and family who are emotionally healthy. You'll know they're emotionally healthy because you feel relatively calm and that you can be yourself when you're around them. Your loved ones will be happy to hear from you. And if they are judgmental or give you issues when you reconnect with them, move along! When you make an effort to spend time around other people, you can rediscover that you can trust others and form friendships that aren't toxic. In this chapter, I'll outline some specific things to watch out for as you're reconnecting socially. I'll also offer you some suggestions for places and ways to find emotionally healthy people who will share your interests and enjoy spending time with you.

"My ex would pit me against other women, telling me that they would hit on him all the time, and other comments meant to stir up my insecurities. As part of my recovery, I am making an effort to build friendships with other women. It makes me realize more and more that a vast majority of people have your back and aren't out to get you."

—Jamie, 28

You Don't Need to Reconnect with Everyone

As you're getting back out there and reconnecting, remember, sometimes we get into toxic relationships because it's what we have known throughout our lives. Not to encourage you to be hypervigilant, but make sure the relationships you're reestablishing are healthy ones.

Are there other people in your life, besides the toxic or abusive individual, who have treated you poorly? Do you know of friends or family members who have disparaged you to others in the past? Was someone too quick to believe a rumor they heard about you—and never bothered to ask you about it? Leave them off your list!

Do some extra vetting of anyone who acted as a flying monkey for the toxic person (as described in Chapter 2). If he carried messages from the toxic person to you after you cut off contact, there's a chance that your abuser is still in his social circle. Or he, himself, may have thrived on that drama. This isn't to say that people can't change. But you should ask. Be direct and clear about that boundary if you decide to reconnect. Many who are recruited to carry messages from abusers to their victims don't realize the harm they are doing. Only you can tell whether your friend or family member is overall a good, healthy person. You aren't looking for perfection—you're looking for someone caring and respectful toward you, who acknowledges and apologizes when he makes a mistake and changes his behavior going forward.

CHECK-IN: IS THIS PERSON HEALTHY?

Do the following statements apply to the friend or relative you want to reach out to?

1. I feel guilted and shamed by this person.
2. This person has told me I need to "earn" my way back into her life.
3. I have been picked on or bullied by this person in the past.
4. I feel drained of energy after I have been around this person.
5. After I have spent time with this person, I question if I am good or deserving of love.
6. They tell me intimate details about other people's lives.
7. This person has threatened to hurt or kill themselves if I end the relationship or friendship.
8. I don't feel like myself when I'm around this person.
9. They have demeaned me, including in front of other people.
10. I feel better when I haven't had contact with them.

If you answered yes to one or more of these statements, you are most likely dealing with a toxic person. Reconsider whether you want to reconnect with this person. Sometimes, it is best to just let that relationship go.

If a person you know threatens suicide, call 911.

Navigating Your New View of Others

After leaving one toxic situation, you may pick up on unhealthy behaviors much more quickly than before. This can lead to all sorts of questions for you: *Am I especially attuned to toxic behaviors? Have they been there all along and I'm just now noticing? Or am I just seeing toxicity in things that are, well, fine?*

Get the answers by asking yourself more questions. Why are you feeling this way? Does it feel as if you are making a healthy connection, or do you have a sense of dread or unease around this person? Is this person showing unhealthy behaviors? As I mentioned in Chapter 5, trust your gut. If something doesn't feel right to you, it probably isn't. Don't stay connected to someone who doesn't have your best interests in mind just because you think you should be "nice." Listen to your intuition. A toxic person may have told you that your intuition was faulty, but it is right on target almost 100 percent of the time. If you need more guidance, revisit the descriptions of unhealthy relationships in Chapter 1 and of secure and insecure attachment styles in Chapter 5. The same criteria that applied to your toxic relationship apply to any person you might spend time with. We'll also cover other red flags and signs of unhealthy dynamics, such as codependency, in Chapter 11.

"Once I learned in therapy what a healthy relationship looked like, I was better able to 'weed out' the toxic people in my life. My life is better because I use less of my energy on people who are not good for me."

—Chandra, 38

Beware of Unhealthy Groups

It may sound alarmist, but I must caution here against a danger you may not have considered. In my practice, I have witnessed vulnerable people leave a toxic situation only to be lured in by unhealthy organizations, such as cults, extremist groups, or multilevel marketing schemes. Keep in mind that we are very vulnerable after exiting a toxic relationship or situation. Our need for connection and belonging may be so strong that we're susceptible.

Leaders of extremist groups zero in on people who are trying to rebuild or heal. Extremist groups know that if someone is feeling vulnerable, she is less likely to question their tactics. Signs of an extremist group include

- Instilling an "us" against "them" mind-set
- Stating they hold "secret" information
- God-like status of the leader
- People in the group are referred to as "followers"
- You are discouraged from seeking information outside the group
- Edicts are only available to "advanced" members of the group
- Sexual exploitation of followers
- You are imprisoned within the confines of the group's buildings
- Threatened with excommunication or violence if you leave

Another form of an unhealthy group is found in multilevel marketing organizations (MLMs). These groups usually require a "buy-in" to participate and usually involve the sale of a product or service. A majority of an MLM's money goes to the people at the very top, while 99 percent of participants lose money.[1] Any company that requires you to pay up front for the "privilege" of selling their products should be looked upon with skepticism. If you have distanced yourself from your toxic family, they may have cut off your financial support. MLMs

> "I finally felt like I belonged somewhere, but I found out that once you joined the group, people never left. They were devoted to the group leader, and people acted like he could do no wrong. I quickly learned that I had unknowingly entered into yet another abusive relationship."
>
> —Kirk, 38

may prey upon people who are vulnerable and may be struggling financially. If you are still considering getting involved with an MLM, check your state attorney general's site for complaints against them. If there is paperwork that the company requires you to sign, ask an attorney to review it for you first. Also make sure the company has a refund policy for products that you haven't sold. The best option is just to not get involved with an MLM.

CHECK-IN: HAVE YOU BECOME INVOLVED IN AN EXTREMIST GROUP OR CULT?

If you are concerned that you may have fallen in with a group of unhealthy people, or if your friends or family members are telling you a group is harmful, see how many of these statements fit.

1. With this group, I finally feel that I belong.
2. The leader has told me I need to give up my possessions.
3. The leader has encouraged me to give financial control to the organization.
4. I am told that I am bad, a sinner, or evil and that the group will heal me.
5. I am encouraged to cut off communication with loved ones not in the group.
6. I am not allowed to ask questions about the leadership of the group.
7. I have been threatened with violence or excommunication.
8. There has been gaslighting from the leader toward the members.
9. There is extreme favoritism toward certain members of the group.
10. We are encouraged to hate a particular group of people.

The more of these statements you agree with, the more likely it is that you've become involved in such a group. Try to contact outside help, whether trusted friends or family members or an authority figure. See Chapter 6 for information on mental health professionals—it is recommended you attend counseling after you leave these types of groups.

Find a Healthy Group

Whether it's a therapy group (see Chapter 6 for a bit more on this!) or an interest group, joining one can help you reconnect with others. One of the best ways to meet new people is through a shared hobby. If you're in a group with a common interest, the conversation may flow more smoothly. If you have social anxiety, joining a group with similar interests can decrease your stress since you can easily discuss something you already know a lot about. (When we are knowledgeable about something, the conversation is less anxiety provoking than if we were talking about a subject that's totally new to us.)

It may feel a little intimidating at first, but be assured that everyone in the group faced some feelings of anxiety when they joined. If you are with a group of healthy people, they should make you feel welcome and your feelings of anxiety should lessen the more you interact with them. If you continue to feel anxiety after meeting with a group multiple times, check in with yourself and see whether the issue is that members of the group aren't emotionally healthy, or that you have issues of anxiety to resolve within yourself.

Other places you can meet people:

- Your neighborhood
- Cultural events
- Classes (dance, cooking, exercise, arts, etc.)
- Online meetup and friend-finding apps
- Book clubs
- Festivals
- Forums
- Gaming
- Running a race
- Dog parks
- Professional networking groups
- Religious groups
- Community centers

- Travel groups
- 12-step groups
- Social activism
- Sports teams
- Nonprofit organizations (Read about the benefits of volunteering in Chapter 10.)

If you would like to socialize with people in a group, it may be up to you to extend an invitation. Try not to worry about being rejected. Being told no can be painful, but it is an inevitable part of life. If someone is not able to get together, that person may have anxiety about socializing, or they may have a lot going on in their lives—it usually has nothing to do with you!

The Pros and Cons of Connecting Online

We're relatively lucky to be living in a modern age where technology makes it so easy to be in contact with our friends and families and to meet new people too. Before social media, many people met others through friends and family. However, that way of making connections is becoming a thing of the past—now, we often meet people directly online.[2] (If you come from a dysfunctional family, you might be wary of meeting someone through them anyway!) While it can be helpful to form connections face-to-face, you *can* also find long-lasting healthy connections via the internet.

There are sites and apps where you can search groups by interest and location. You can also find support groups, including 12-step groups for recovering from dysfunctional parents, families, or other loved ones. See whether there is a group that matches your interests and needs. Do try to meet up in person at some point, as seeing people in person can help strengthen friendships, particularly in the early stages.[3]

There are some pitfalls to using the internet or apps to meet people. If you have connected with people online, keep track of the time you spend doing so. Going online can eat into your time quickly, and, as mentioned in the last chapter, spending a lot of time on social media can worsen feelings of depression and anxiety. One boundary you can set is having good time management and being able to prioritize. Setting a timer can help you remember when to shut off being online.

Be careful that the people you are talking with are who they say they are. Don't give out any personal information. Keep in mind that you are vulnerable right now, and some people can sense that and prey on it. So, if you meet up with someone you met online, bring someone else with you and always meet in a public place.

Remember, as I briefly mentioned in Chapter 5, there's really no substitute for phone calls and face-to-face contact when it comes to building emotional intimacy. To help rebuild positive connections to healthy people, meeting and communicating online can be a good starting point, but I urge you to get back out there and meet up in the real world.

Reintroducing Yourself

When you reconnect with a friend or family member, it can be challenging to know what to say. There has been so much that has happened, yet you find it difficult to know where to start. Consider the following when "reintroducing" yourself.

"I know we haven't been in contact much recently. I hope you and I can rebuild our relationship. If I have hurt you in any way, I apologize. Can we start again?"

That's what worked for Jules (from the beginning of the chapter). She decided to call her mom first, figuring that a family member might be easier to reestablish a relationship with. She went to see her mother on a Saturday figuring a weekend would be a less stressful time for both of them. They both cried and shared a big hug. This gave Jules the courage to call Meghan. Like Jules, just take things a step at a time.

The way you deliver this statement depends on your relationship. How did you primarily communicate before? Sometimes, sending a text can be easier than saying it over the phone or in person, but you miss out on a lot of nonverbal communication. It's understandable if you want to reach out in a less direct way, especially if you are concerned about being rejected. For these first contacts, whichever way you feel is best is the right way. If the other person takes offense to how you reached out to her, reconsider if you really want a relationship with that person.

Be aware that nothing says a person has to accept your apology and reconnect. Sometimes, for various reasons, people aren't going to accept an invitation to rekindle a relationship with you. Know that this has nothing to do with you, even if it feels deeply personal. Sometimes, people have a "one strike, you're out" policy when it comes to relationships. It's not a healthy way to go through life, but it serves a purpose for that person by not allowing herself to get hurt. However, it also means that she misses out on rekindling friendships, such as with you. Remember, how people treat you says more about them than it says about you.

> "I was nervous about reconnecting with my sister, but when we started talking, it was like no time had passed."
>
> —Maria, 54

What You Should and Shouldn't Apologize For

When you reconnect with loved ones, you may feel a sense of wanting to say you're sorry for everything that has happened between the two of you. It is entirely normal to feel that way. However, apologizing for things that aren't your fault can set up an unhealthy dynamic in your relationship. You may have been used to apologizing profusely to your toxic partner, boss, or friend.

Things you shouldn't apologize for include how you feel, maintaining a boundary, or upholding your rights as a person (if you need a refresher on this, revisit Chapter 5).

When should you apologize to someone?

- When you have made a mistake in how you have treated someone
- When you have provided false information to someone, knowingly or unknowingly
- When you have lied to someone, knowingly or unknowingly

- When you have behaved in a way that is contrary to your beliefs and values
- When someone tells you that you have hurt them
- When you have offended someone
- When you have omitted information that the person had a right to know or would have been helpful to them

When you're feeling an urge to say sorry, ask yourself whether an apology is needed. That doesn't mean you shouldn't apologize when you have hurt someone; it means that there are many times in life when we use apologies when they aren't really needed or appropriate.

Sometimes, an apology should be a statement. For example, "I'm sorry to take up your time" could be more assertively said as "Thank you for being patient"; "I'm sorry my opinion is different than yours" could be rephrased as "Thank you for listening to my side of the story." When you reframe an apology as a statement, you are more assertive and standing up for yourself.

"I Feel" Statements

When you need to share your concerns or feelings or set a boundary with someone, an "I" statement or "I feel" statement is a way of informing someone without blaming him. You may have heard of these—they're a standby recommendation of family therapists and relationship counselors, and for good reason. This is the basic structure of an "I feel" statement:

When (event happens), I feel (emotion) because _____. I think that we should (solution).

For example, "When I call, and my call isn't answered for a few weeks, I feel anxious because I feel as if I have done something wrong. I think it might be a good idea that we keep in contact once a week."

When using the "I feel" statement, the key is to avoid using the pronoun *you* because the other person can feel blamed and get defensive. Instead, by stating *your* needs and what *you* would like to see happen, you have a better chance of having a constructive dialogue with the other person about your feelings and concerns. If you are concerned about the conversation being awkward, stating the obvious, "This is really awkward, but . . .," beforehand can help everyone feel more comfortable.

By stating your proposed solution with the pronoun *we*, you are clearly inviting her to participate in forming a solution. You are also letting her know that the answer is a team effort—it's the two of you against the issue, not against each other.

Keep in mind that using the "I feel" statement is not a guarantee that the other person will be open to hearing your concern or work on a solution with you. But you will know that you tried, and not wanting to cooperate with you is her issue, not yours.

JOURNAL PROMPT: PREPARING YOUR "I FEEL" STATEMENTS

You most likely have relationships where you would like to bring up an issue but are not sure how to do it without awkwardness, or you are concerned the other person will judge you. When you practice writing out what you are going to say to someone, it can make the actual event much less stressful. Think of someone with whom you generally get along well, but there has been a sticking point for you that has been hard to let go of. For a roommate or partner, it may bother you that they leave toothpaste on the sink. While you could clean it up yourself, you are getting irritated by that, and just want her to do it herself. First, ask yourself whether it is a reasonable request. Yes, adults should be able to clean off the bathroom sink as an act of courtesy and respect for their living space. Next, write down how to address this issue using an "I feel" format. For example, "When toothpaste is left on the bathroom counter, I feel frustrated because I like having a clean counter and I don't want to get toothpaste on myself. How about we each do a quick clean of the counter when we're done in the bathroom?"

Now it's your turn! Write out some "I feel" sentences about issues you may be having in your relationships. Sometimes, people have no idea that something is bothering you unless you take the step to say something about it. You can role-play the possible interaction with another trusted friend or relative so you can fine-tune your communication and desensitize yourself to the actual conversation.

Feeling Defensive with Others

When someone tells you that your behavior bothered her, it can be tough to take. This can be especially true if a toxic person constantly belittled you. One criticism, and you feel that you are back at square one. Know that your reaction may be solely because you received nothing but criticism from the toxic person.

The way you're feeling is entirely understandable. You're taking big steps toward healing, and you might feel vulnerable for many reasons—it's only natural that you want to protect yourself while you still feel emotionally fragile. It's important to remember that not everyone is toxic. It may feel like it at first, but you can and will meet healthy people. Healthy people may bring up concerns with their friends and loved ones because that is what healthy people do: openly address issues and conflicts so that they can be resolved, and no one is left resenting the other person. Open communication (that's transparent but not brutal) helps people grow outside their comfort zones.

It is good that someone cares and is mature enough to address a problem with you, granted that it is done in a kind and courteous manner. Constructive criticism is when a person handles a situation using kindness. An example of a healthy concern might be, "The tone of voice you used this morning made me uncomfortable. Can we talk about it?"

If you were defensive, you might say, "I have no idea what you are talking about," or "No, we're not going to talk about it." Instead, a healthy response is "I'm sorry I hurt you—yes, let's talk." Know that even if you disagree with how someone is feeling, he has a right to those feelings.

CHECK-IN: ARE YOU FEELING DEFENSIVE?

With how many of these statements do you agree?

1. When someone tells me that I have upset them, I automatically feel that they have no right to do so.
2. When I receive constructive criticism, I think to myself that the person is a jerk.
3. I hold grudges after people have told me they are upset with me.
4. I avoid other people so I don't have to deal with possible criticism.
5. I have quit a job or activity after being given constructive criticism.
6. I have reacted to criticism with yelling or screaming.
7. I have left the room in anger or avoidance after someone addressed a concern with me.
8. I have spoken badly about someone to others after that person addressed a concern with me.
9. When I receive criticism, I almost immediately start crying.
10. When someone brings up an issue, I make a joke about it.

If you answered yes to one or more of these statements, you might be using a defense mechanism to protect yourself. If you need assistance in overcoming fear or anger in reaction to constructive criticism, talk to your therapist about it. She might even be able to role-play some conversations with you so that you can practice a caring and non-defensive response in a neutral environment.

Surround Yourself with a Support Team

Because you may have been isolated from your friends and family, you may not have been able to build up a support network. It's essential you have people you can talk to if you run into issues throughout your life (and everyone does!). Even if you aren't feeling particularly social or just don't like people, it helps to have at least one person in your life with whom you can process ideas and concerns. The ideal support person is someone you can call any time—even at three a.m. when you are in crisis. (Just keep in mind that it is a good idea to extend that same courtesy to them!)

You may already have a support network and just don't realize it due to your previous isolation. Look for people at work, in your neighborhood, online, or at your place of worship that you already turn to for support. You may have more help available to you than you realize. Write those people down on a list to reach for when you need to talk to someone. If you can't think of anyone that is in your support network, that's okay. Look for people who accept you for who you are and who are also good listeners.

JOURNAL PROMPT: DISCOVER YOUR SUPPORT NETWORK

Like Jules at the beginning of this chapter, you may now feel that you are out in the world on your own without much support. However, your network may be larger than you think. Get out a large sheet of paper and draw a bull's-eye—three concentric circles. In the middle of the circle, write down the people whom you could contact at any time, even at three a.m., if you needed something. In the next circle out, write down the names of people whom you would feel comfortable calling during the day, but either don't know them well enough yet or know that they have limitations that exclude calls late at night. In the outermost circle, write down acquaintances—people you bump into sometimes at the store, people at your house of worship, the people you wouldn't necessarily refer to as "friends," but you like them. Now, step back and count the number of people you have written down. Take a picture of the bull's-eye and mark it as a favorite on your phone. Take a look at it when you are feeling alone or you are needing some social contact. Consider getting to know some of the people in your outer circles, and work on maintaining healthy relationships with the people in the center of the bull's-eye. You can transfer these names into your journal as well.

Give Up Attachment to Outcomes

A final word on reconnecting: Give up your attachment to the outcome. This means not putting pressure on yourself (and others) to make that connection happen. Instead, look at what you are learning from the experience.

For example, you may have learned that even after being isolated from people, you are doing pretty well at getting back in the swing of things. You may have rediscovered your confidence. You probably stretched outside your comfort zone. Success leads to more success. How the other person responded doesn't have any bearing on your ability to connect with others; the most important thing is that you attempted. Be very proud of that.

· · · · ·

In this chapter, we explored why reconnecting with people you were isolated from is an essential part of healing. An unhealthy person separates you from family and friends to gain control over you. However, you can reconnect with your family and friends and also forge new connections. You learned what to do about feelings of anxiety and dread about reconnecting with the people in your life. You also discovered ways to meet new people, especially if you now realize the people in your life are toxic.

Having a support system is vital right now because being able to reach out to others can be very helpful when you're navigating feelings of grief and loss. That's what we'll cover in the next chapter.

9

GRIEVE

How to Work Through Loss So You Can Heal

ONE OF THE FIRST FEELINGS PEOPLE HAVE WHEN THEY LEAVE A TOXIC
relationship is a feeling of overwhelming relief. It can feel like finally being free. But with the end of any relationship also comes grief.

Grief is a difficult thing to process, even if you have experienced a
healthy relationship. Add a toxic person to the mix, and it can feel like
torment. It can also be confusing because you feel you've made the right
decision to cut this person out of your life—and you're still distraught.
While you are grieving, you may be feeling a variety of emotions, sometimes all at once. Feelings of relief, frustration, anger, rage, anxiety, gid-
diness, and sadness are all completely normal.

There is so much that makes grief complicated after a toxic relationship. You felt attachment and love toward that person, as unhealthy as he
might have been. It doesn't mean anything is wrong with you—it means
you are human and have experienced a loss. What's more, you are grieving not only the loss of your relationship but also the friend or partner
you thought you knew; your grief is compounded by the fact that the person you entered into a relationship with is not the person they turned out
to be. Toxic people can have a very adept way of looking like something
they aren't. Toxic people start showing their true selves while you are

already in a relationship, and when that mask of niceness and loving behavior drops for the first time, it can be quite a shock.

You may be grieving the fact that you have to coparent with a high-conflict person for the rest of your life. You may have quit your job, the one you worked so hard for, because it was just too unhealthy for you to stay. You may be experiencing multiple losses at once if you need to stop contact with your family of origin for the sake of your mental health. You may have several life transitions happening at once.

You may also be grieving who *you* were before the toxic relationship or situation changed you. You may have smiled more and felt calmer before you met him or her, or before your friendship turned sour. You can be that person again, even a better version of that person. But it does take some time to heal.

Go at Your Own Pace

You may want to shake off grief as fast as you can. It can feel pretty terrible. However, grief is a funny thing—the more you try to let go of it, the more it sinks its claws into you.

You may have heard of grief being described as like being hit by huge waves. You are hit constantly at first, then over time, the waves get smaller, and you are knocked down for shorter periods. Once in a while, a massive wave of grief will hit you out of nowhere. These giant waves of grief can show up when you run into your ex or former boss or watch a show that brings up issues about toxic relationships. If a toxic person has died, you have the finality of her death, but you can still remember her as you go about your life. Sometimes, you won't know what triggered the memory. The point is that healing from grief and loss is a continual process.

There is really no reliable timetable for grief. Anyone that tells you that there is a specific time frame when you should start "feeling better" or start dating again doesn't know the depth or brevity of your grief. People may tell you either that it is too early to start dating or that you have been grieving "long enough." Don't let anyone judge or rush you. Only you can say what's right for you.

You may need to sit with your grief or talk through it to get to the other side. Otherwise, you may sublimate your grief into unhealthy behaviors, such as addiction. It can be helpful to talk to a mental health professional who can guide you through the grieving process. If you aren't already working with a therapist, please revisit Chapter 6, where I outline how to find a provider and pay for your sessions. It's a worthwhile investment, especially while you're working through grief.

The Kübler-Ross Stages of Grief

You may have heard of the five stages of grief: denial, bargaining, anger, depression, and acceptance. This is a model that psychiatrist Elisabeth Kübler-Ross introduced in the late 1960s, and it's now commonly referenced in pop culture. These stages of grief apply whenever you experience any loss, whether it is a breakup, death, decrease in health, or loss of a dream. Although we often think of these stages as a common, linear process, you don't necessarily go through these stages in any particular order—and you may experience more than one at a time. You may even skip stages or go back through stages. It is simply a framework for what you might encounter and helps people see that the process of grief, while unique to each person, is also universal. Knowing that everyone in the world experiences grief at some time can help you feel not so alone.

Shock and Denial

You can't believe your relationship is over. If a toxic person broke up with you, you might have dissociated when you were told things were over. Dissociation happens when you feel like you aren't present. Your brain "checks out." If you left the relationship, you might have felt elation as you drove away. You may feel very little guilt or remorse.

Bargaining

You tell yourself you'll do anything to be back in the relationship. If you believe in a higher power, you may pray or even beg that you will give something up if your former friend or partner would come back. You may wish you could trade your new job for the one you had.

Anger

Your anger during the grief process may be directed toward yourself, your ex, or a friend or family member. You may be angry that you spent so much time in the situation or that you were treated poorly and unfairly. You may be angry that you didn't speak up more during the relationship (even though speaking up could have led to injury). You may be mad at family and friends who encouraged you to leave the relationship.

Depression

You may have difficulty getting out of bed or have no interest in things that used to engage you. Depression doesn't always look like sadness—it can also feel like your feelings have been muted to the point where you don't feel anything.

In depression, some people may think of hurting or killing themselves. If this happens to you, contact a mental health professional. You can also contact the National Suicide Prevention Lifeline at 1-800-273-8255 or suicidepreventionlifeline.org.

Acceptance

You have come to terms with the fact that your relationship has ended. You know that you eventually will be okay, entering into a new normal for your life and feeling more like yourself again. While acceptance may be seen as a good place to be in the grieving process, it doesn't mean that you are entirely free from grief or that you can't return to an earlier stage—and that is completely normal. You have grown and are making progress.

Complicated Grief

The five stages of grief end with acceptance, and embracing a "new normal" is generally what happens. However, what if the feelings of loss don't seem to go away or get better with time, but instead they gnaw at you and it's hard to think about anything else? This is what mental health professionals refer to as "complicated grief," and it happens to a small percentage of people who are grieving (between 7 and 10 percent). It is grief that is above and beyond what a person is reasonably expected to feel after a loss. In complicated grief, the brain reacts to a loss similarly to how it would react to suddenly quitting an addictive substance.[1]

Many times, people who have had trauma from toxic people or relationships develop complicated grief because, as we discussed in earlier chapters, a toxic person might still be trying to get you back and you can't get closure. When you have complicated grief, you may experience one of the following:

- Excessive worry
- Obsessive thoughts
- Avoiding locations that remind you of your loss
- Using substances or other addictive behaviors to avoid feeling grief
- Mood swings
- Suppressing or holding in emotions
- Inability to accept the loss
- Difficulty practicing self-care or hygiene
- Difficulty envisioning a meaningful life or future without the person
- Deep feelings of anger
- Difficulty managing daily activities
- Thoughts of suicide

Some factors increase your risk of developing complicated grief. If you already have depression and/or anxiety, substance abuse issues, physical health issues, feelings of dependency on others, feelings of guilt, a perceived lack of social support, or family conflict, you might be at risk.[2] You may also be more likely to experience complicated grief if you have a negative view of yourself and had a hostile or conflicted relationship with the person you have lost—so, a toxic relationship by its nature can make you more susceptible.[3]

"When I needed to stop contact with my family due to their denial of the abuse I endured, I felt I was experiencing grief the way other people did. But then it took what I call a 'sharp turn' and I felt debilitated. I wound up not eating for days and felt like I was going to die from heartache. Luckily a good friend leveled with me and said that my grief seemed more intense than other peoples', and I needed to get help."

—Victor, 40

If you are experiencing grief that seems to not ease up or is causing you difficulties with day-to-day functioning, talk to a mental health professional who specializes in grief and loss (revisit Chapter 6 if you need more support on this).

Living Loss and Ambiguous Loss

If you had to cut off friends or family members due to toxic behavior, you most likely are grieving over people who are still alive—which can make your grief feel incomplete and never ending. When people experience grief that is not due to a death, it is called a *living*, or *ambiguous, loss*.

With ambiguous loss, you may be left in a sort of limbo. The person isn't dead, so you may hold on to hope that they will someday come back to you or that the situation will change. Or, even if you don't want to see them again, you might have to because you have children or work together. This complicates the grieving process; it's harder to finally accept that the relationship has ended and move on with your life.

As we explored in Chapter 3, sometimes you need to achieve closure on your own or come to terms with the fact that you may never get the closure you want. The following jour-

"How am I supposed to get any kind of healing when I see him every other day?"

—Chandra, 28

nal prompt is another way to process these experiences and find some peaceful feelings.

JOURNAL PROMPT: CREATING YOUR OWN ENDING

When you don't get the ending that you wanted or needed to a relationship or situation, you can create your own ending. Write down the details of the toxic relationship, including how it ended. Now, write the rest of the story. What will you accomplish now that you no longer have an emotionally unhealthy relationship? What will you have time for now that you didn't before because you spent time anticipating what the other person wanted? How will you grow from this experience? Maybe you'll be able to travel places or do activities that otherwise were "off-limits" because the toxic person didn't approve. Write down all the ways that you will become a better person from this experience.

When a Toxic Person Has Died

Jessie grew up with three sisters and a mother who would pit the girls against one another. Her mom and sisters saw her as a "bad kid" because she often got in trouble for acting out at school. Her mother would punish her even more but meanwhile lavish her sisters with praise and gifts.

One Christmas, Jessie excitedly raced downstairs and looked under the tree. To her shock, she didn't get anything—while it seemed that her sisters had gotten even more presents than usual. Jessie started crying. "Suck it up," her mother said coldly. "Why were you expecting anything when you've been such a problem child?" Jessie never forgot what it felt like to hear those words.

As Jessie grew into adulthood, she had less contact with her mother and sisters. With her therapist's help, Jessie saw that she wasn't to blame for how her mother had treated her. In her early twenties, she finally cut off all communication with them.

Five years later, she got a call from a number she didn't recognize. It was one of her sisters. Her sister said that their mother was dying and that Jessie had "one more chance to do right by Mom."

Jessie felt that she was being thrown back into the role of the "bad kid" again. She was conflicted—part of her wanted to have nothing to do with her mother or her sisters, while part of her wanted some type of closure. So, Jessie decided she would visit once more to say good-bye to her mother.

When she arrived at her mother's room in the hospital, she was shocked at how different her mother looked. In Jessie's memory, her mother was a large, imposing figure. Now she looked smaller, curled up in a hospital bed. Jessie held her breath—she'd half hoped her mother would apologize for the way she'd treated Jessie for all those years. But her mother took one look at her and sneered, "Oh, look, how blessed we are by your appearance." Jessie stayed for a half hour before she couldn't take any more barbed comments. Feeling angry but oddly crushed, Jessie drove away from the hospital and straight back home.

When she met with her therapist later that week, Jessie broke down into tears. Her therapist said, "Jessie, even if things didn't turn out the way you wanted, you made an effort. You did what you felt was right. I don't mean to be blunt, but please remember, bad events don't make mean people into better people." She also talked with Jessie about what a brave, healthy, and independent woman Jessie had become despite her upbringing.

Jessie didn't attend her mother's funeral and went on a long-awaited trip instead. Jessie is still working through her grief over her relationship with her mother and sisters but feels peace.

Like Jessie, you may have had a toxic parent or partner die—and you are feeling very conflicted. You feel a loss, but not like your friends experienced when their emotionally healthy parent or partner died. You also grieve the parent or partner you should have had, one that supported you and truly loved you. Feeling conflicted or having contradictory feelings about a toxic person that passed away is completely normal. You may feel anger, relief, sadness, disappointment, elation, and many more feelings, sometimes all at once. You may remember good times, followed by memories that you'd rather erase altogether. Journaling and talking about your experiences with that person, especially with a mental health professional (MHP), can be very useful in sorting through your feelings and expressing them. The more you process through your grief by talking, writing, or expressing it in other ways, the less chance you have of developing complicated grief.

"When someone says to me, 'She's in a better place,' I don't want her to be in a better place. She made my life hell. But telling someone you're glad your mother is dead is not really what you're supposed to say."

—June, 22

JOURNAL PROMPT: PROCESS FEELINGS ABOUT A DECEASED FRIEND OR FAMILY MEMBER

Are you angry, sad, disappointed, relieved—or all these? Write down the feelings that you are experiencing in this moment, as many as possible. As you write, don't judge yourself for what you are writing; there's no right or wrong way to feel when someone who caused you pain dies. As you go through the grieving process, make a point of redoing this exercise. If you feel you are in a rut with your grieving, review what you wrote weeks or months earlier. You may find that you have experienced more personal growth than you thought.

JOURNAL PROMPT: WRITING A LETTER TO THE DECEASED PERSON

Because you are no longer able to tell the toxic person how they have impacted your life, it can help to write your feelings down in a letter format. Write to the person about your memories of her, how she impacted your life, and how she changed the way you view the world around you—anything you still want to say to her. Also write down how you have healed from her legacy of unhealthy behavior. You can either keep the letter in your journal to review it as you are further along the grieving process, or you can symbolically let it go by shredding it, tearing it up by hand and throwing it out, or burning it.

Grief over Quitting Your Job

If you left your job because a toxic person made your work life miserable, you may have given up a job that put you on a great career path. Even though leaving your job is worth decreasing emotional and physical stress, you are still faced with a loss. It is very unfair that another person's behavior made you give up a hard-won opportunity.

One of the best ways to heal is to start looking for new employment. Get in contact with people whom you enjoyed working with in the past and see whether their company is hiring. Before joining a new company, ask former and current employees about their experiences. Some people have left toxic work environments and gone into business for themselves as consultants or even as a competitor to their former company. Check your employee agreement to see whether you have a noncompete clause. Consult with an attorney if you are unsure if you are able to work for a competitor due to your contract.

You may consider switching fields. A career counselor is a licensed MHP who has additional training in helping discover what careers may fit you best. She can also help you work through this grief, talk about how your job impacted your well-being or self-esteem, or how past life events have influenced your choice of career. You can meet with a career counselor either in person or online—either format is equally effective.[*] You may also find a support group helpful. Ask a career counselor whether they know of any groups that are specific to people who have experienced a toxic work environment. If you're looking for a career counselor, know that this is *not* the same as a job coach. A job coach can help you with your résumé or practice interviewing, but he is not a licensed MHP and as such is not trained to help you with the deeper issues of grief.

"I thought I was making a great career choice. Instead, I got a boss who tormented me. I had to leave, and I feel like there has been no justice."

—Maricela, 35

JOURNAL PROMPT: REVIEWING YOUR TOXIC WORK EXPERIENCE

It may be helpful for you to write out what you experienced at your toxic workplace. When we write out traumatic experiences, it can help us process them and get to the point where we can consider letting those thoughts go. Writing out your experiences doesn't make the events disappear from your memory, but it can make those unpleasant memories less intrusive and more manageable.

You can also write down what you enjoyed about your job so you know what to look for in the future. Maybe your boss was a bully, but you liked working in a team with your coworkers. You may have had a coworker that sabotaged your work, but you felt the company was a good match for your values. Also write down what you learned from the experience. If you are seeing a career counselor, consider sharing what you have written in order for the counselor to best help you.

Grieving in Coparenting

When you are coparenting with a high-conflict person, you may experience different levels of grief and stress. You are grieving over the healthy, functioning relationship you thought you were going to have. Your coparent may be a person that you don't recognize anymore. She certainly isn't the person you first met and knew in the early stages of your relationship. You may be grieving the parent that you feel your children truly deserve. You may be angry toward not only your coparent but also yourself. If you are battling trying to forgive yourself, see Chapter 4.

Although it can be tough to acknowledge or admit, you might also be grieving the fact that you even had children with this person. If you are regretting being a parent, you are not alone. Many people are hesitant to talk about it for fear of looking like a "bad parent" or being judged. It is not something that is talked about openly, and it probably should be. Being overwhelmed and thrown into a coparenting situation, possibly not by your choice, can lead to many conflicting feelings. You have a right to your feelings, even ones that feel scary and unkind.

Working through coparenting grief on your own can affect your relationship with your coparent and even your children. You might want to speak with a mental health professional specializing in coparenting issues with a high-conflict person. A mental health professional can help guide you in handling issues with the coparent as they arise.

"If I had known then what I know now, I wouldn't have even gone on a first date with him. Now I have to deal with him the rest of my life."

—Mariel, 40

In addition to a mental health professional, a parenting coordinator may make coparenting easier with a high-conflict coparent. For more information on parent coordinators, see Chapters 1 and 5.

CHECK-IN: COPARENTING WITH A HIGH-CONFLICT PERSON

Answer yes or no to the following statements:

1. I find myself resenting my children.
2. I have anger toward my coparent more days than not.
3. I am questioning my ability as a parent after interactions with my coparent.
4. I wish my coparent would fall off the face of the earth.
5. I have found myself not wanting my children to spend time with their coparent.
6. Most of my interactions with my coparent result in fighting.
7. I feel my coparent is harassing me.
8. My coparent is withholding child support from me.
9. I feel my coparent is constantly testing the boundaries of our parenting plan.
10. It is difficult for me not to speak badly about my coparent in front of our children.

If you answered yes to any of these statements, consider seeking the guidance of a mental health professional and a parent coordinator. Many coparents of high-conflict people have experienced these same feelings and more. Getting support for a difficult situation, such as coparenting with a toxic person, may help you and your children reach a place of stability even when the coparent acts out.

Support Yourself Through Grief

In addition to working through grief with your therapist, there are things you can do to help create a nurturing environment in which to heal. Connect to others who can comfort you and make sure that your needs are met.

Let Others Know

While you are going through grief, let trusted friends and family know. If you are working at reestablishing connections after your toxic relationship, revisit the last chapter for some guidance; you want to be especially sure that you're surrounding yourself with healthy people while you're grieving. Tell others what you need, whether it is someone to listen or help formulate solutions, or just to be left alone. If you don't know what you need, let your loved ones know that too. You aren't expected to know what you want while you are on the roller-coaster ride of grief.

Let friends and family know that you don't want to talk about the toxic person or situation unless you bring it up first. Having family and friends bring up the person may impede your healing process. When you tell people ahead of time that you won't be talking about the person unless you bring him up, it decreases the chances of harmful comments from others.

Sometimes, people say stupid things to you while you're grieving, mainly because they are at a loss for words. What they say may be well-intentioned, but their words can still hurt. You already feel like a raw nerve, and trusted friends and family that seem to judge you on handling your grief can feel very painful.

Sometimes, it can be difficult to tell whether someone was well-intentioned with the stupid thing they said or malicious. Look at the person's pattern of behavior. Is this a person who has said rude, insensitive, or cruel things in the past? If so, she may be a toxic person you just need to stay away from without leaving her with a parting comment. If it is a person who has appeared to act in your best interests in the past, it may be helpful to say to her, "I know you are just trying to help. Saying that

I need or don't need to do something while I am hurting is causing me more harm than good. What I need right now is just someone to listen." By stating the issue and what you need, you are being proactive and focusing on where you and your friend or family member can go from here.

Maintain Healthy Boundaries

Setting boundaries with others is essential at this time. As do many who have left toxic situations, you may feel that you don't have good boundaries. You most likely have had good boundaries throughout your life—they may have just been systematically dismantled in this particular relationship or situation. One of the best ways you can take care of yourself is by saying no. Remember, "no" is a complete sentence. While it is more socially acceptable to say, "No, but thank you for asking," you are not required to say why you are turning down a request. Revisit Chapter 5 if you'd like more guidance on reestablishing boundaries.

Prioritize Your Self-Care Routine

Taking time for yourself is crucial when you are grieving. You need to put your health, emotional and physical, above all else to heal. When you feel better physically, such as when you get enough sleep and engage in exercise, you are more likely to feel better mentally and emotionally. Exercise even reduces inflammation and neuroinflammation that can trigger major depressive disorder.[5] Sleep disruptions can occur when you are experiencing anxiety and post-traumatic stress disorder (PTSD).[6]

Treat yourself as you would treat your best friend—this practice of self-compassion can help us make a rough day a little easier, gives us permission to rest when we need it, and can provide us with motivation to push forward. If you need it, take another look at Chapter 7, which has many suggestions for ways to practice self-care.

In addition to getting exercise, consider joining a support group, attending therapy, and journaling. Many people find that creating something, whether through woodworking, painting, or any other hands-on activity, helps with calming the mind while they are experiencing grief.

And sometimes you just need to feel the feelings to get through them. When you are in the throes of grief, remind yourself that as bad as this feeling is, it is temporary. There will be days when you feel better.

Get Involved

As you begin to feel more balanced and are moving on with your life, get involved by volunteering for a group or cause that you believe in. Not only can keeping busy (within healthy limits) help you manage grief, but it can also help you reconnect with people, see the good in life, and develop a sense of purpose and meaning.

• • • • •

When you experience any kind of loss, you go through a grieving process. However, when an unhealthy relationship or situation is involved, your grief can be more intense and complicated. While accepting your loss is the ultimate goal, grieving a toxic person, particularly one who is still alive, can be nerve-wracking. In this chapter, we explored strategies to weather your grief until you feel more yourself again. When you feel ready, volunteering can help you rekindle your sense of purpose in life. In the next chapter, you'll find out just why volunteering can be such a great choice and get some ideas on how to get involved.

10

VOLUNTEER

How to Reclaim Your Purpose Through Altruism

Y OU'VE COME A LONG WAY TOWARD HEALING FROM YOUR TOXIC RELA-
 tionship. You've blocked or minimized contact and established
boundaries. Perhaps you're making good progress working with a therapist. You may have reconnected with friends and family you hadn't
spent much time with. You're giving yourself time to grieve. You've been
treating yourself with love and forgiveness, and you've prioritized self-
care. So, this next step in the healing process may take you by surprise:
volunteering—really?

You may feel that you don't have the time or energy to volunteer, especially right now. But going out into your community and giving the
gift of your time is truly one of the best ways to rebuild your life. When
you are in crisis, asking "How can I help?" can be a very powerful action.
When you help others, you also help yourself. Why? Well, volunteering
has many benefits that will help you through your healing process. It reminds you that you have worth and a purpose in life. It's an excellent way
to connect with your community and meet new people. It reminds you of
your passions in life. And, on a very basic level, it offers you a healthy way
to stay busy.

In addition to exploring these benefits, in this chapter you'll learn how to find volunteer opportunities as well as important things to keep in mind.

Are You Ready to Volunteer?

If you feel you don't have the time or energy to add volunteering to your schedule, I get it. We all lead busy lives, and when you're working through grief, you may feel drained, physically and emotionally. You may also feel that you can't undertake another attempt at being strong since you have already had to be too strong to survive emotionally.

However, empathy and altruism are strongly related to resilience in the face of stress; working to build this compassion for others can help you build inner strength.[1] What's more, you already have shown that you are resilient, so the chances are good that you also have a high level of altruism. Altruism is the act of helping others without expecting anything in return. Intentionally practicing altruism and empathy can help increase your resilience and life satisfaction.

Cultivating a sense of compassion for others through volunteering can help create a "cushion" between ourselves and the trauma we have endured.[2] This is especially important if the toxic situation you were in has left you feeling cynical and down about how much power you have to change your life. When you are volunteering, you see in real time how you are helping others. When we help others, we help ourselves. When you are giving the gift of your time, it increases your level of life satisfaction.[3] You may have been a generous person long before you were in a toxic relationship or situation. If a toxic partner forbade you from participating in any independent activities, it may have caused you to have feelings of anger and grief. If you were exceptionally altruistic, not being able to help others can especially cause such issues as anxiety and depression.[4]

A caveat here. You may find that you overschedule yourself because it has been so long since you had complete control of your time. So that you don't cut into time for rest and self-care, you may want to ease into volunteering, especially if you are learning how to reestablish boundaries and reassert your rights and wants as a person. (Therapy and other introspective work, like journaling, can help.)

"Being around people who are working toward a common goal helped me focus outside what was going on in my life."

—Debra, 56

Keep Busy

At a basic level, volunteering your time gives you a healthy and productive way to stay busy, which helps you through the healing process. Having some sense of structure in your day can help reduce anxiety and depression. What's more, when you are helping others, it can provide a welcome distraction to cut down on the amount of time you think about your current situation. Sometimes, when you have been through something traumatic, you will *ruminate* about it—you will think about it over and over and won't be able to let it go. When you are busy helping others, you may find that your mind naturally lets go of what is bothering you. Freeing your mind from the past, even temporarily, can help you be more open to experiencing new things and meeting new people.

That said, it's important to strike the right balance so that you can process your emotions and work through grief, as we covered in the last chapter. Be honest with yourself about your motivation for getting involved. Are you filling your schedule to keep busy so you can avoid ever feeling the pain of grief? While being busy can be helpful in building your life back up again and keep you distracted, it is important to sit with your feelings and experience them.

Consider volunteering for a limited number of hours and see how that fits into your life. You can always increase the amount of hours later!

"Most of my day was spent thinking about my ex and what he put me through. When I started volunteering, I found that the time went by quicker, and he didn't take up as much space in my mind."

—Sherry, 50

Find Your Purpose and Rebuild Your Self-Worth

Toxic people have a way of belittling you to the point where you give up on who you wanted to be and what you wanted to do with your life. You might also be struggling with low self-esteem or self-worth, as if you don't have much to contribute to your own well-being or to the world around you.

Volunteering reminds us all that we do have worth, and every one of us has a lot to give. You have something to contribute, even if you feel you may not have anything to offer. Your skills and your time are valuable, and nothing makes that clearer than putting them to use for good. When you give to others through volunteering, you also gain insight into your purpose in life. Finding meaning in life, in large part, is about contributing to your community or people.

It's important to keep in mind that when you've left a toxic situation you may not regain your self-esteem right away—it will be a series of baby steps to rebuilding. Connecting with others through volunteering is a great way to take those small steps toward independence. The more you successfully accomplish on your own, the more it builds up your self-esteem. It also shows you that you are capable of not only helping others but helping yourself as well. You may find that your overall health improves when you are volunteering—not just your mental health but your physical health too.[5] Volunteering has been shown to increase self-efficacy and self-esteem.[6] The more you are feeling better about yourself, the more time and energy you have to further improve your quality of life.

If you've left a toxic workplace and are currently looking for employment or taking a break from working, volunteering can be a great way to fill the gap. Sometimes, volunteering leads to opportunities you otherwise might not have seen. You're building a network of people who may be able to help you find a new job. Volunteering after you have left your job gives you something positive to put on your résumé. It's also better to say that you spent your time volunteering after quitting your job than to explain why there is a gap on your résumé.

> "When I cut off contact with my toxic family, I felt like I didn't have anything to contribute to anyone. Now I am surrounding myself with people who tell me how much I am helping, and that makes me feel really good."
>
> —Joshua, 26

Reconnect and Help Yourself out of Isolation

As we discussed in earlier chapters, toxic situations can be extremely isolating. If you view yourself and people around you as all being part of a greater plan, it may help you feel more connected to society in general. When you are giving your time and energy, you are helping connect with others around you, whether they are people or animals.

If you haven't felt ready to be very social just yet, you can choose how exposed you want to be to others by where and how you volunteer. If you'd like a slow ramp-up to social contact, seek out volunteer opportunities where you can do office work or other work with limited face-to-face contact. You can work your way up to more in-person interactions as your trust in people grows.

Importantly, volunteering reminds us that we are not alone. When you've just gotten out of a toxic situation, it can feel as if you are the only one who has experienced that kind of abuse. You may even feel that everyone is better off than you. When you volunteer with people in need, it helps you realize that we all have difficulties. You are not alone in your suffering. While you might think that would be depressing, it can be life-affirming to see other people who experience hardship showing resilience.

Rediscover Your Passions and Find New Interests

Alma always enjoyed sewing. She remembered her grandmother's teaching her when she was a young girl. It was a way for her to express herself, and she would regularly gift her work to family and friends. She sewed a quilt for her boyfriend, Liam. During one of their many arguments, Liam told her that the quilt was ugly, that quilts were "for old ladies," and it looked as if the amount of time she had spent on it was equivalent to the amount of time she had spent on their relationship—"like almost zero effort." Alma stopped sewing after that. Just looking at her sewing machine reminded her of Liam's verbal abuse.

One day after Alma finally left Liam, she walked over to her sewing machine and took off the cover. It had been at least two years since she last used it. It was like reconnecting with an old friend. Day by day, Alma started getting back into sewing again, reconnecting with a long-hidden part of herself. She also felt that she was reconnecting with her family through sewing as she remembered the wonderful times she spent with her grandmother at the sewing machine. Alma decided she wanted to share her sewing knowledge with others. Alma found an organization that taught sewing to women who had survived domestic violence and were learning a new marketable skill. Alma thought this was a perfect fit—she could share her love of sewing with others, and she would be helping other women gain skills and independence. And most of all, she felt a sense of pride and connection that she was teaching others as her grandmother had taught her long ago.

Did you, like Alma, have an interest or passion that your toxic ex-partner, friends, or family ridiculed you about or stopped you from pursuing?

Now is the time to start again or even try something new. You don't have to answer to anyone, so just enjoy your time. Volunteer experiences can be opportunities to bring you back in touch with your passions in life or try new things with limited risk to you. Volunteering is a great way to learn skills. If you're volunteering for something, the organization is invested in teaching you the best way you can help them. Research some organizations that may be a good fit for you based on your passions and skills. For instance, if you love animals and are a skilled writer, contact a local shelter to see whether it could use help writing inviting bios for pets awaiting adoption.

"My ex told me that my hobbies were 'stupid' and taking away from time that I should have been spending on him. From volunteering, I've learned that there are a lot of other people who share the same interests as me."

—Janice, 70

How to Get Involved

By now, I hope you see why I recommend volunteering—like almost nothing else, it can help you heal and grow. So, now let's talk a little bit about how to do it.

There are so many ways to get involved, and I think you'll get the most satisfaction by spending time doing something that you genuinely enjoy or that makes a difference for a cause or issue that's important to you. So, what ideas might that give you? Do you have a particular interest, such as animal welfare? Or do you like working with a specific age group? Here are some ideas to get you started:

- Run a donation drive to collect items for a food pantry, shelter, or school.
- Help your neighbors with day-to-day needs, such as walking kids to and from school, caring for an elderly neighbor's lawn, walking dogs, or taking photos during events.
- Give blood or plasma.
- Tutor at a school or give free lessons in something you're skilled at.
- Chaperone a field trip.
- Look for volunteer opportunities at a library, community center, animal shelter, performing arts organization, or food pantry.
- Reach out to a local organization where you can mentor children.
- Become a docent or guide at a local museum or historical site.

Check online with a site that specializes in listing volunteer opportunities (see Resources, page 224). Also, ask trusted friends and family for recommendations.

Scheduling Volunteer Opportunities

You need not volunteer with an organization—there are plenty of ways to do community service on your own (for example, picking up grocery orders for your neighbor who is sick or donating some craft supplies to a local elementary school). That said, joining an existing organization makes it much easier for you to connect with others and make new friends. If you do decide to get involved with an organization, look at what kind of time investment they want from a volunteer, and make sure it fits your schedule. Now is an excellent time to establish boundaries about what you are interested in doing, how you will give your time, and how many hours per week you want to dedicate to volunteering.

Find a Mentor

When you are volunteering, you may find a person who exemplifies what you would like to be when you feel back to yourself again. Having a mentor can help you through the growing process. You may already have someone in your life that you look up to and would like to get some guidance from them on your journey to wellness. There are organizations that match you up with mentors based on your interests. You can also contact someone you know or a professional connection to ask her if she could help you along the path of building up your career experience, including volunteering. That's what Elena did after her divorce.

Elena was understandably nervous about going back into the workforce. The last time she had had a full-time job was when she was pregnant with her first son twenty years ago! Her attorney recommended an organization for women reentering the workforce after a life transition. The organization would help Elena with her résumé, provide her information on jobs that matched her skill set, and offer a support group for women like her. What's more, it offered Elena the opportunity to have a mentor; she would be matched up with someone who best fit her interests and field of work.

Elena looked forward to being matched up with a woman who was currently an executive administrator just as she had been. She wanted to know how her job had changed in the past two decades. One day not long after, an executive administrator named Fatime left a voicemail for Elena. They had been matched up for the mentoring program. Although she was initially nervous to meet her, her future mentor's warm demeanor on the phone put her at ease, and Elena made arrangements to meet Fatime at her office. They talked about what Elena's job had been like, her family, and what her ideal position would be now. They also talked about Fatime's job, and she gave Elena a tour of the office. Elena found that while the technology aspect of the job had changed quite a bit, she knew she was a quick learner! Fatime and Elena agreed to meet up once a month and talk via a messaging app about once a week. Having a mentor answer her questions helped her to address some of her fears.

If you are volunteering to get back into the workforce eventually, a mentor can also act as a liaison between you and people who might hire you. It can be helpful to "shadow" someone who has a job or interest similar to yours. *Shadowing* someone means you are accompanying them in their workday or volunteer hours to understand better what they do and whether you would like to pursue the same line of work. To shadow someone, simply ask if you can. Most professionals know what shadowing means. If asking someone to shadow them is intimidating, you can just ask them questions about their work.

A mentor can also be a good "mirror" for the behaviors you would like to see in yourself. Make sure your mentor is emotionally healthy. You can observe how your mentor interacts with her boss and the people on her team. Does she speak respectfully and with kindness while also establishing healthy boundaries? How does she deal with conflict? Having a good role model is invaluable, especially when you are relearning how to set healthy boundaries and interact assertively with others.

Become an Advocate

If you're ready for it, one of the best ways you can turn your negative experiences into a positive is to educate and support others who have been in toxic relationships. Ways to advocate for others include

- Leading a support group
- Speaking about your experiences
- Writing articles, a blog, or a book about your experiences

Keep in mind that before you can help others, it is essential that you have worked through your issues from your past toxic relationships— best done with the help of a good therapist. This is because if you haven't taken care of your issues, others' sharing their stories can trigger your trauma—something called *vicarious traumatization.*

Preventing Vicarious Traumatization

If you are working or volunteering with people who have been through trauma, such as a toxic relationship, you may be prone to vicarious trauma, where hearing about others' experiences triggers you to relive some aspects of your own past. It's also known by the names *secondary traumatic stress* and *compassion fatigue* (when you feel exhausted and unable to feel compassion for others). You may start taking on someone's trauma as your own, experiencing a heightened level of stress and a marked change in how you perceive others and the world around you. Anyone who helps people who have been through trauma may be susceptible to vicarious traumatization, but you may be even more so if you have a history of trauma yourself, whether from a toxic relationship or a history of abuse and neglect. You are also more likely to experience vicarious trauma if you work in a helping profession, such as counseling or nursing, or feel a strong sense of empathy toward others.[7] Signs of vicarious trauma include

- Nightmares about a client's trauma
- Anger and sadness that don't subside
- Difficulty feeling any emotions (numbing)
- Becoming too emotionally involved or invested in clients' lives
- Experiencing guilt and shame about clients' experiences
- Difficulty with obsessive thoughts about clients' lives and issues
- Taking on a cynical view of others or others' intentions
- Being hypervigilant (having a strong startle response)
- Insomnia related to thinking about client issues
- Feeling trapped or wanting to flee
- Avoiding being alone
- Looking for routes of escape
- Viewing most people as having severe trauma

- Withdrawal from others
- Exaggerated perception of crime in your area
- Feeling hopeless about the state of the world or your clients' situations
- Transferring feelings about clients' perpetrators onto your partner and getting angry or avoiding contact with your partner
- Being overly protective of your children

If you feel that you may be experiencing vicarious trauma through your volunteer work or job, please speak to the supervisor at your volunteer site. You may need to scale back your hours or work in another area of the organization where you are less likely to engage with people who have experienced trauma. Your advocacy organization should have support available if you have started experiencing flashbacks or other signs of reexperiencing trauma—for instance, an organization that helps victims of domestic violence or other forms of abuse should have steps in place for when volunteers or employees experience a resurgence of their trauma. If your advocacy organization does not have any help available, ask it for a referral. (Then, reconsider volunteering with that agency again.) In either case, you may need to take a step back from volunteering with that organization while you work through the reoccurrence of your trauma. Remember that this is a regular occurrence when working with people who have gone through the same abuse as you.

Remind yourself that you are only responsible for yourself and your feelings. The person you're working with should be working harder than you at resolving her issues. You may be able to offer tools and support, but it's not your job to "fix" an issue for her. Also be realistic about what you do and don't have control over, and how much you can help. It may be encouraging to look for the small changes that clients are making rather than to expect them to have an epiphany and make sweeping changes.

It's a good idea to meet with a mental health professional (MHP) regularly when you are working with people who have experienced trauma.

Talking through traumatic memories with an MHP can help you process them so that flashbacks happen less often.

Practicing proactive self-care is another essential part of preventing vicarious trauma, so be sure to revisit the practices in Chapter 7 as you're volunteering.

"Eventually, I'd like to be an advocate for people who have been through narcissistic abuse. First, I need to sort through some of my stuff with a therapist."

—Joe, 32

Have a "buddy system" with another volunteer where you can check in with each other. You should also have a supervisor of volunteers who meets with you on a regular basis. In addition, keep a journal of your experiences so you can review it for potential signs of retraumatization.

JOURNAL PROMPT: TRACK POTENTIAL SIGNS OF BURNOUT

When you are working in a toxic environment or are working with people who have been traumatized, you may experience burnout. Burnout happens when you feel you no longer have anything to give and that you don't have anything to look forward to.

Other signs of burnout include
- Difficulty getting up in the morning
- Having a depressed, angry, or anxious mood most of the day
- Feeling that you aren't helping anyone
- Insomnia or hypersomnia (sleeping too much)
- Binge eating or restrictive eating
- Feelings of distrust or even hatred toward coworkers and clients
- Becoming cynical (assuming that all people are only interested in themselves)
- Feeling exhausted
- Not taking breaks during the day
- Feeling isolated, or isolating yourself from others
- Wanting to run away or escape

- More frequent illnesses or flare-ups of chronic medical conditions
- Lack of enjoyment in leisure activities
- Lack of motivation
- Feeling despondent, that things aren't going to get better

Many times signs of burnout can sneak up on us. Every day, write in your journal how you are feeling. Use a scale of 1 to 10 to measure your level of hopefulness and purpose. A 1 would indicate you are feeling that you don't make a difference at all, and life has little meaning for you. A 10 would indicate that you are feeling very hopeful for the future and you feel you are connected to your life's purpose. It is perfectly normal to have a range on that 1 to 10 scale from day to day—but pay attention to when the number is consistently low, or if you go from a 1 one day to a 10 the next day. Fluctuating often between extreme highs and lows can be a sign of a mood disorder or working in an unhealthy environment. At the end of the week and end of the month, review what you have written. Do you see any patterns? Are there certain days, tasks, or people who tend to increase or decrease your feelings of hopefulness and purpose? Pay attention to those details and see how you may be able to change your circumstances.

Disclosing Your Trauma in a Public Forum

While sharing your experiences with a toxic person or situation can help others, be cautious about revealing any identifying information about your ex-partner, friend, relative, or workplace. It is usually best to speak in general terms about the relationship or situation rather than use names, locations, time frames, or details about appearance.

You may be tempted to give out that information to protect or warn others who might meet up with the toxic person. Posting specifically about your ex, friend, or coworker creates a reason for them to contact you, which you really don't want. If you're writing about your experiences in a public forum, be aware that legal issues could also arise; for instance, the toxic person could accuse you of libel (which is writing false information about someone that caused them harm). You also need to be careful if you have kids, to protect their right to privacy. When you are posting about your experiences, an excellent guideline to go by is "Would I want my kids to read this?" If they aren't able to read the content now, they may when they are older. Consider consulting with an attorney to verify and get good confirmation that the information you are writing about won't get you in legal trouble.

What's more, chances are that the toxic person has told his new partner, his friends, or his family that you are "crazy" or "unstable." Someone who is in the toxic person's life will most likely not listen to your advice even if they did see it. Unfortunately, they may have to learn about his pathological behavior the hard way. You may feel sorry for those people—that is a normal feeling, but it doesn't mean you have to act on it. It is not your job to "fix" someone else's situation. Sometimes, you can help more people when you keep your experiences more general, as people will more likely identify a situation as being similar to their own when your posts don't get into specific detail.

Make Sure You're Volunteering for a Healthy Organization

Make sure the organization you are considering volunteering for engages in ethical practices. You want to avoid getting into another toxic situation if possible—and, if you find yourself in one (which is just part of life sometimes!), you want to recognize it and extract yourself from it as soon as possible.

Research about the organization online. Who is on the board of directors? Has anyone in the organization gotten in trouble for illegal or unethical behavior? Has the organization had any complaints filed against it? What was the outcome of the complaint? How much of the money the organization raises goes to the people or animals that it says it supports? For information about how a charity's money is being used, search for that organization on www.charitywatch.org.

When you've satisfied yourself that an organization is healthy, remember that you still need to look out for healthy and unhealthy *people* within it—such behaviors as love-bombing and triangulation (described in Chapter 1) can happen in any group. Listen to your intuition. If you are talking with someone and something feels off, pay attention to that feeling. If you are looking to volunteer at a location, look at how people interact there. How do the volunteers speak to one another? How does the head of the organization treat others with less power? How does the organization treat its clients? People should all be treated the same, with respect and dignity. If you hear people at the organization ridiculing or bullying others, either to their face or behind their back, get out of the volunteering situation as soon as possible. You may also need to report any unethical behavior.

If you see anything that doesn't feel right to you, cut your ties with that organization and move on. If you aren't sure if what you saw or heard is unhealthy, talk about it with a trusted family member or friend to get their opinion of it.

"I looked up the background of everyone on the board of directors and also the supervisor of volunteers. If any of them had been accused of harassment, I would have refused to volunteer there."

—Jane, 34

CHECK-IN: ARE YOU VOLUNTEERING WITH A HEALTHY ORGANIZATION?

When you are volunteering, it's essential to know whether the organization has any kind of dysfunction. You want to make sure that you are rebuilding by being around healthy people and a healthy system. Note whether any of the following is happening where you are volunteering.

1. You can change your hours, with notice, without being guilted or shamed.
2. You are encouraged to talk to someone if you feel that your role isn't a good fit.
3. You believe in the organization's core values.
4. The leader and supervisors of the organization treat volunteers and those that they serve with respect.
5. The organization's activities are safe and don't put you in uncomfortable situations.

6. You have received training from the organization before volunteering.

7. A supervisor is available at all times on-site or at the volunteering location.

8. The organization does regular check-ins to see how things are going for its volunteers.

9. If there is a change in time, place, or venue, you are notified in a reasonable amount of time.

10. A vast majority of the money raised by the organization is used for helping the population served.

The more statements you identified as happening in the organization, the healthier your volunteer placement. If you only found one or two of these statements to be true of your organization, it may be time to move on to a healthier one.

· · · · ·

Giving your time to help others can, in turn, help you: it provides a healthy distraction, connection with others, and a sense of purpose. You find yourself connected to something larger than yourself.

You may consider eventually advocating for others who have been affected by toxic relationships. Make sure you are not retraumatizing yourself if you are working with others who have experienced unhealthy relationships. One of the most important aspects of volunteering and giving back is making sure you surround yourself with healthy people; in this chapter, you also learned how to recognize signs you've gotten involved with an unhealthy organization. Toxic people and situations can be anywhere, even within seemingly admirable, mission-driven organizations. Now that you've come so far with your healing, in the next chapter, we'll explore how to recognize these dynamics and prevent them from developing in your future.

11

PREVENT

How to Avoid Toxic Situations and Set Yourself
Up for Healthy Relationships

MEKE WAS NERVOUS ABOUT HER FIRST FORAY BACK INTO THE DATING
world after a ten-year relationship filled with toxicity. Meke had
taken a few months to regroup, go to therapy, and get to know herself
again, eventually coming to realize that she didn't do anything wrong,
and that nothing justifies abusive treatment. But now, here she was again,
on the dating scene and terrified of meeting someone like her ex, Tomasz.

Meke started messaging with some of the men she met on dating
apps. It felt so strange (partly because many of these apps hadn't even
existed the last time she was single!). Some of the people she messaged
were pushing too quickly to meet in person; with others, she felt that
she was being strung along. But then she found Miles. The two seemed
to click instantly: they both liked travel, cooking, and dogs. After they
had been messaging for a couple of days and had a phone call, Meke felt
ready to meet him in person. At their first dinner date, things were going well . . . until Miles got upset at their server for bringing the wrong
food. Meke wanted to hide under the table from embarrassment. But
then she thought, *Maybe Miles is nervous about the date. And maybe I'm just*

overreacting after what happened with Tomasz. The rest of the date went well, and both Meke and Miles looked forward to seeing each other again.

Miles was late to their next date—and didn't call or text to say why. Meke was torn between annoyance and worry. When he finally showed up thirty minutes later, he said, "There was a lot of traffic and I didn't want to text from the car." Meke was unsure: on a second date, how much should she say about how his lateness and lack of notifying her made her feel? Lateness aside, Miles had so much going for him—he was a great listener and they had so much in common. As they were walking to their cars, Miles started telling Meke about his traumatic childhood. It seemed like way too much information too soon. "Miles, I appreciate that you feel comfortable telling me about your past, but I'd like to take things slower," she said.

Miles stopped, looking stunned. "Uh, okay, no problem," he replied, his expression changing from pain to a happy smile in a second. The quick change in emotions took Meke aback, and she wondered if she missed any other red flags. Was Miles toxic? Or was he just awkward?

• • • • •

Like Meke, you've come a long way since you left your toxic situation. Now, you may be wondering how to navigate future relationships, knowing that toxic people tend to prey upon people who care about others.

Your empathy and caring are beautiful traits! There is nothing wrong with opening your heart to others. Just do it with an added layer of protection. You will rebuild—and your life can be better than ever.

Remember the Signs of a Toxic Relationship or Situation

Educating yourself about toxic people and relationships can help you heal and prepare yourself for meeting new people. Pay attention to the red flags of potential abuse the next time you meet someone. Remember, as we discussed in Chapter 1, a pathological pattern repeats itself in almost every toxic relationship: they idealize you, then devalue you, and finally discard you.

In unhealthy relationships, toxic people often love-bomb you at the beginning. Other signs of idealizing include

- The person says that she has never met anyone like you before.
- She mentions that she has been treated poorly in the past and you are the first person that has treated her well.
- She describes you with superlatives.
- She pushes for moving in together on a date or at the beginning of a relationship.
- Your interests are so alike it is almost frightening (the toxic person is "mirroring" you).
- You are hired on the spot for a job that usually would require a more thorough vetting process.
- She starts dressing like you or picking up your mannerisms.
- She wants to occupy most of your free time.
- She discloses all her dysfunctional history when you first meet "because you are so easy to talk to."

When Miles started telling Meke about his troubled childhood, she remembered her therapist talking about *trauma dump*, when a toxic person divulges too much of their history of trauma too soon. Although it's a clear sign that they don't have solid boundaries, sometimes people mistake it for emotional intimacy and feel good that a person was willing to confide in them. But there is a means to an end. It's a way that toxic people often try to bond and get others to "attach" to them. Meke recognized this sign and asked Miles to take things slow. Many idealizing behaviors feel like flattery, but they're really an effort to take up more and more of your time and isolate you from other people in your life.

Once a toxic person knows you are hooked and are deep in the relationship, he slowly starts the cycle of emotional abuse with devaluing. Where you once could do no wrong, now you can do no right. Signs of devaluing by a toxic person include

- Picking on things you can't change, such as your body or your voice
- Comparing you unfavorably to others (exes, friends, family members, or other employees)
- Pointing out small errors
- Bringing up "mistakes" you made months and years ago
- Sabotaging your work
- Ridiculing you in front of others
- Blaming you for not participating in an activity that he planned without notifying you
- Using stonewalling or the silent treatment
- Making comments about her supposed superiority to you
- Showing up late or not at all to dates or other events
- Blaming you for her behavior
- Using your chronic health issues against you or ridiculing you about them
- Telling you that you are crazy or that other people think you are crazy
- Pitting you against your friends, other coworkers, or family members by telling you they said unkind things about you (also known as triangulating)

Then, they drop you, leaving just as quickly as they entered your life—this is the discard process. They may still keep you in the background in case their new narcissistic supply no longer meets their needs. Signs of discarding by a toxic person include

- Stonewalling for an extended period of time
- Abandoning you at a location away from home
- Having a relationship outside yours
- Abruptly firing you from your job
- Telling you not to come back due to some perceived slight
- Leaving your belongings outside your shared residence and changing the locks

- Moving on to new narcissistic supply, such as a new partner or new friend
- Hoovering you by drawing you back in, only to discard you again

When you meet someone for the first time and experience idealizing behaviors, consider whether this is a strong enough warning sign to not continue contact with this person. If you feel that the behavior is curious but that it is not severe enough to warrant discontinuing contact, file it away as "data collection." If the person continues to show you any of the listed behaviors, end the relationship immediately, go no contact or low contact, or start seeking other employment.

"He couldn't get enough of me in the beginning, and then two months later he was telling me how stupid and crazy I was. Naturally, I blamed myself. Now I know this is a pattern he has had in other relationships."

—Desiree, 60

If You Go Back

When you leave a toxic relationship or situation, remember that the person may try to hoover you, or suck you back into having contact with them. As soon as you go back, the same dynamics will return.

Remember that the person's behavior doesn't change without her doing a lot of introspective work, like the kind that is done in therapy. If you do decide to reconnect, keep a healthy distance from the person until you see evidence of real change—repeated healthy patterns of behavior toward others, reacting maturely when a person or event doesn't meet their expectations, or a letting go of expectations altogether. Other signs of change include no longer bringing up the past and accepting no the first time you say it. A person who has made changes in their behavior takes responsibility for her actions, and apologizes when it's appropriate.

While you may feel flattered or wanted, hoovering is not about loving you—it is about power and control. Even if your ex promises you that things will be different this time and that he or she has changed, don't take those words at face value. Violence in a relationship, including emotional abuse, almost always escalates. Pay attention to what your ex does more than what he says. Also, pay attention to your feelings. You may feel a sense of anxiety and dread or experience flashbacks to abuse during the relationship. Know that if you resume contact with a toxic ex, you have a greater chance of being seriously injured or killed.

If you decide to return to a toxic workplace, make sure there are parameters in place to help you protect yourself. Don't stay alone at the office or when there are only a few people left. Document your concerns, and have your workspace moved to another floor or away from the toxic coworker. If you were working with a toxic supervisor, by all means, request a change. The ideal is to look for signs the company is committed to ending toxicity. For example, the company has hired an industrial or organizational psychologist to determine what protocols and aspects of the company culture need to change—and followed through with them. See whether the board of directors or other people in charge have been replaced with people who look out for the rights of others. Healthy workplaces have a written protocol for reporting harassment, and cases of harassment and bullying are dealt with quickly. If you find that your rights continue to be violated at your place of employment, consider reporting it to human resources (if available at your workplace), and start looking for another job.

"He promised me the world, so I went back. After a week, things were worse than they were before."

—Alex, 28

CHECK-IN: HAS THE TOXIC PERSON IN YOUR LIFE TRULY CHANGED?

If a toxic person in your life is trying to reestablish contact with you, ask yourself the following questions:

1. Is the person hesitant to attend counseling or work on his behavior in other ways, such as in a support group?
2. Has the person taken responsibility for their behaviors toward you and others?
3. Has the person apologized for ways they have hurt you?

4. When you address your concerns with this person, are they truly listening to you, or do they get defensive?

5. Is the person promising you precisely what you were lacking or wanting in the relationship, so much so that it seems too good to be true?

6. Is the person promising you that things will be different this time, but provides no evidence of change?

7. Is the person going overboard trying to hoover or get you back with constant texting, phone calls, or stopping by your house unannounced?

8. When you refused to resume the relationship, did the person respond with anger and attempts to guilt and shame you?

9. Did the person try to get to you by sending messages through your friends and family?

10. Have you blocked the toxic person's email, phone numbers, and social media, yet he still finds a way to reach you?

The more questions you answered yes to, the greater the chance that this person is still showing the same toxic behaviors he had when you were together. Proceed with great caution and consider cutting off contact again.

Be Kind to Yourself

If you are tempted to return, or if you have taken steps to reconcile, remember to practice self-compassion. This person has told you all the things you want to hear—who wouldn't want to go back to someone who promised the world? Having self-compassion also means that you know that your priority is to take care of yourself, which means not returning to a toxic and potentially lethal situation.

If you are out in the dating world, chances are you will run into a toxic person. You may feel overly cautious or that you are not being fair by analyzing a person's behavior for toxic traits. You may also find yourself falling for an unhealthy person again. Practicing self-compassion is very important during the dating process. Otherwise, you will spend time berating yourself for falling for another inappropriate person instead of taking this as a learning experience. Maybe you noticed early on that this person was not emotionally healthy or good for you, and you broke things off. That is progress, and you should be proud of yourself for taking that step.

Build the Foundations for Healthier Relationships

There are entire sections of bookstores devoted to advice on building strong relationships, whether with romantic partners, family, friends, or colleagues. That's not my goal with this book—I want to keep the focus primarily on *you* and how you can heal. However, having healthy connections to people around you is a big part of a fulfilling life. And those who have survived toxic relationships and situations may be particularly susceptible to a few common missteps when entering into new ones. In the rest of this chapter, let's explore how to protect your emotions, get clear on what you want, and learn healthy ways of interacting so you can set yourself up for success in the future.

Remember Your Attachment Style

As you read in Chapter 5, there are different styles of attachment to others—secure, anxious, avoidant, and disorganized. Your attachment style can influence whether you continue a relationship or stay in a situation that is unhealthy for you.

With anxious attachment, you may have a fear of abandonment, and you continue contact with someone who is unhealthy because you feel it is better than being alone. With avoidant attachment, you may be drawn to unhealthy people because they may not let you close to them, which suits your need to be more detached emotionally. With disorganized attachment, you may experience a mix of anxious and avoidant impulses, making maintaining a relationship very difficult—and a toxic person's idealizing behaviors all the more attractive.

If you have a secure attachment style, you are more likely to quickly recognize unhealthy behavior in a person, so you can take a step back and assess whether this is a one-off occurrence or a sign of a bigger issue.

That is not to say that securely attached people can always identify idealizing behavior—covert narcissists can be very good at hiding pathological behavior early on in a relationship and have fooled many people into believing they were emotionally healthy.

As you're navigating your new relationships, if you haven't already, revisit the check-in in Chapter 5 that helps you identify your attachment style. Remember, there's nothing wrong with starting with an insecure attachment style. The important thing is to be aware of your patterns—and remember you can break them to move toward secure attachment.

Look at People for What They Are, Not Their Potential

When meeting others, especially when dating, many of us tend to look at a person's potential rather than what they are at that moment. While it's optimistic and hopeful to look for what someone could be, you are not a fix-it shop. It is not your job, nor is it healthy, to try to mold someone into who you want them to be. Look at who they are at this moment. When we look at someone's potential rather than who she is in the moment, we may be subconsciously trying to "fix" that person. Doing so is unhealthy and can result in resentment and disappointment from you, and frustration from your friend and partner.

"I've gotten into toxic relationships because I thought, 'He just needs someone to love him.' Now, I look to see if he's already done the work to make himself an emotionally healthy person."

—Vivi, 40

JOURNAL PROMPT: REALITY VERSUS POTENTIAL

Think about a toxic relationship that you were in, where you stayed in it because you were looking at someone's potential rather than who they were at that time. Write down where you saw potential in the person, and then describe what the person was really like. How much of a difference was there between what you thought the person could be and what he turned out to be? How much did your need to "fix" play into looking at potential instead of reality? Embrace your ability to see potential in others, but also keep it in check when it clouds your judgment in relationships.

Make a List of What You Are Looking For

Sometimes, we know what we *don't* want in a friend or partner, but we haven't clearly stated what we want. Take the time to make a list of what you are looking for in a person. Get as specific as possible. Try not to judge or criticize yourself while you are making the list. Items may include

- Gets along well with my kids
- Likes animals
- Gets regular checkups
- Wise spending habits
- Speaks respectfully to me and others
- Sense of humor
- Kind to others
- Equal give-and-take in the friendship
- Open communication
- Has other healthy relationships
- Has healthy boundaries and respects others' boundaries
- Compatible values

Try to frame items on your list as positives. Instead of "Doesn't interrupt me," consider writing "Waits until I finish speaking." Instead of "Doesn't yell," consider writing "Respectfully speaks to me."

When you meet someone that you want to get to know better, read over your list. Also, read over your list when you move from dating to relationship status. Sometimes, infatuation or love makes us not think logically. Go through your list and see how many items fit your potential

mate or new friend. If he doesn't meet some criteria, review how important those items are to you. It may be that the person you are with gives
you butterflies, but you may not match up in values or sense of humor.
Remember that it's a myth that there is
just one person in the world that is a perfect match for you. You'll meet people who
are more compatible with you than others.
It's just not possible for one person to meet
all your needs.

> "When I thought I had found 'the one,'
> I took a look at my list. It turns out my
> emotions were overruling my sanity."
>
> —James, 48

There should be an equal give-and-take in a relationship, including
friendships. A toxic person may do all the taking in a relationship, while
you end up doing all the giving. Granted, there are times when there
may be a temporary imbalance, such as when a friend is sick or she has
a family emergency. If you feel that there is more of a permanent imbalance in the relationship, have a talk with your friend. Sometimes, when
you start an awkward conversation with "This is awkward, but . . ." it
makes it a lot easier to talk about the situation. If it feels as though the
issue is still not resolved, consider scaling back the time you two spend
together, or decrease the amount of favors you are giving. In cases where
you get a gut feeling that the relationship isn't healthy, you may need to
cut off contact.

Making a list like this doesn't only apply to relationships—it goes for
jobs too. Those criteria may include

- My supervisor is kind and provides positive feedback.
- My questions are answered respectfully.
- I know what is expected of me.
- I look forward to going to work.
- There are perks, such as medical benefits, flex time, or working
  from home.
- I find the work interesting.
- I feel valued by my employer.
- I am helping other people.

- Guidelines and expectations are consistent.
- The company's culture is consistent with my values.

You may not know at the beginning whether your job matches some of the items on your list. However, the fact that you wrote down what you are looking for in an ideal job means that you will be more aware of your needs and wants, and will be tipped off to any concerns at an earlier stage.

Know the Right Time to Be Vulnerable

Vulnerabilities are any experiences or feelings that trigger deep emotions in us—sadness, joy, grief, or anger. They are sensitive things that we wouldn't share with a stranger. They may make us embarrassed or uncomfortable, as though we're different or don't fit in.

Being vulnerable with someone is a choice. A toxic person will gather information about your vulnerabilities and use them against you in the future—this is known as using *emotional ammunition*. Toxic people will remember things you told them long ago and will pull that vulnerability out when they want to keep you off-kilter. For instance, if you once confided in a toxic person that one of your biggest fears is not being liked at work, he might say to you during a fight, "No wonder no one at work likes you!"

Is a new friend or date asking you very personal questions right after you meet? These might be questions like

- What are your deepest fears?
- What are your biggest regrets?
- Who have you let down the most in your life?
- What have been your most significant losses in life?

It may feel like you are building emotional intimacy with someone by answering these questions. Sometimes, you can get swept up in feeling connected to someone and start sharing personal information right away. But when you ask those questions back, a toxic person will deflect or come up with an answer that seems not genuine.

Make sure the person you are vulnerable with is worthy of it. It doesn't mean you need to put up a wall with everyone! It means that you need to be selective about with whom you share your feelings and fears, and when you do it. Sometimes, people feel that if they are not vulnerable with someone, they are cold or unfeeling, but that is simply untrue. You need to be kind and loving toward yourself first—and sometimes that means waiting before deciding to share personal information.

CHECK-IN: IS THIS PERSON WORTHY OF MY VULNERABILITY?

If you're not sure whether someone will treat you with respect when you open up to him or her, consider your answers to the following questions and statements.

1. Has this person shown themselves to be trustworthy?
2. Have they treated me with respect?
3. Have they treated others with respect when they were vulnerable?
4. They respect and honor anything sensitive that I've told them.
5. They know my tender spots and treat them with care.
6. They are kind to children, pets, and any other living thing that is more vulnerable than the general population.
7. Do they genuinely listen to me?
8. Do they ask how I am doing and listen to the answer?
9. Do I feel safe around this person?
10. Would I want my children or parents to meet this person?

If you answered no to any of these questions or statements, the person might be toxic. Proceed with caution. If you answered yes to many of the questions or statements, the person may be one that you can trust when you share your feelings and thoughts. However, still proceed with cautious optimism until this person has earned your vulnerability through continued trustworthy behavior. If you are unsure if a person can be trusted, it is best to wait and not divulge personal information.

Break the Pattern of Codependent Behavior

When you're building a new relationship after a toxic one, it can be very easy to fall back into *codependent* patterns. Codependent behavior happens when you depend too much on your partner or other people in your life for emotional stability, validation, or a sense of purpose. In codependency, your moods and behavior are highly dependent on the other person's. You don't feel okay unless he feels okay. If he is upset, your life goes into a tailspin trying to make him feel better.

In essence, if you are codependent, you feel responsible for other people's feelings or problems. You are willing to sacrifice your own well-being to take care of them. There is a difference between offering someone support and hurting yourself to make them feel better. For example, if your friend is depressed, you might encourage her to see a mental health professional. But if your friend says she will only go if you pay for the sessions, you'd be doing yourself and her a disservice if you agree. As another example, say your mother needs a ride to her doctor's appointment, but she told you only a few hours ahead of time. If you don't have anything planned and it doesn't interrupt your schedule or cause any other consequences, driving her might be a reasonable (if slightly aggravating) favor. But if taking her would make you late to work, and you do it anyway, that's putting her needs over your own and veers into a codependent response.

You're more likely to develop codependent behavior if your partner, family member, or friend has an active addiction of any kind or has untreated mental or physical health issues. When a person doesn't take steps to heal his own issues, it can lead to a cycle of a loved one—you—trying to "fix" the problem. It is not your responsibility to fix anyone, and trying to solve someone's problem for him can lead to resentment on both sides. A person needs to want to change his behavior. We can't do it for him.

If you choose to have a relationship with someone who refuses to take responsibility for his issues, consider practicing loving detachment.

Loving detachment is a concept whereby you can support someone who is struggling with issues while also prioritizing your mental health and self-care. You can still care about him and encourage him to get help, but you remember you're not responsible for his choices. You maintain a clear boundary between his pathological behavior and your right to a happy and peaceful existence.

"I really relate to the saying, 'I will no longer set myself on fire to keep you warm.'"

—Diego, 36

CHECK-IN: IS YOUR RELATIONSHIP CODEPENDENT?

Count the number of statements with which you agree.

1. I base my feelings on how someone else is feeling.
2. I find myself ignoring my needs to focus on another person's needs.
3. I relate to the saying "Setting yourself on fire to keep someone else warm."
4. I stay up late to make sure the person hasn't been drinking or using.
5. I have helped a person with his addictions even after he has stolen from me or caused me harm.
6. I feel that my only chance at having a relationship or happy life is to stay with this person.
7. I would stay in this relationship no matter what happens.
8. I make excuses for this person when they behave in a toxic manner.
9. I have started using substances or other addictive behaviors to cope with the stress of this relationship.
10. I avoid conflict at all costs with this person.

If you agreed with one or more of these statements, you might be in a codependent relationship. Speak with a mental health professional to learn about codependency and setting healthy boundaries; if you need help finding one, revisit Chapter 6.

JOURNAL PROMPT: CONFRONTING CODEPENDENCY

You may have had a pattern of codependency in previous relationships, whether they be at home, at work, or in friendships. Take time to write down the signs of codependency you have had in the past. Write out in detail what you might have been feeling or thinking when you tried to compensate for someone's toxic behavior. For example, if the toxic person in your life had anger management issues, you may have had a habit of apologizing on behalf of that person or tried to smooth over his relationships with others.

Next, write down what you expect from people in your life now. To continue the previous example, you might expect that a person will not exhibit anger control issues. If he does, you expect him to make a conscious effort to improve.

If you are confronted again with inappropriate behavior by this new person in your life, write down what you will and will not do. If a loved one has an outburst of anger, you will not placate him or apologize on his behalf. You will also practice detachment and let him solve his own relationship issues that occurred as a result of his anger.

When we confront the codependent behaviors we have had in the past, we are more aware of when those behaviors might be sneaking back into our lives. When we confront those behaviors from the beginning of a new relationship, we are able to change course more quickly and thoroughly.

Make Sure You Both Make Equal Effort in the Relationship

If you feel that you are putting in considerably more effort to sustain a relationship, or prioritizing the relationship to the detriment of other areas of your life, take a step back and see if your dynamic is healthy or not. Putting in more work than your partner, family member, or friend may be a sign of codependency.

**CHECK-IN: ARE YOU PUTTING TOO MUCH
EFFORT INTO A RELATIONSHIP?**

Answer yes or no to the following questions.

1. Are you initiating most of the contact (texts, phone calls, etc.)?
2. Do you feel that you are the one who has to rearrange your schedule to accommodate last-minute changes by your partner, friend, or family?
3. Does your partner, friend, family member, or coworker tell you that you need to be more accommodating?
4. Does your partner change plans on you at the last minute?
5. Do you check in with your partner about their feelings, but he or she doesn't ask you how you are feeling?
6. Are your phone calls and texts rarely answered or answered after a significant amount of time?
7. Have your friends and family commented that it seems like you are putting more effort into the relationship than your partner?
8. Does this person come home late without explanation or show up at your house or office unexpectedly?
9. Has this person asked you for money and has a history of not paying you back?
10. Has your partner, friend, or family member expected you to pay every time you go out?

The more questions you answered yes to, the more likely you are in a relationship where you are putting forth more effort than the other person. If the other person isn't willing to talk about this and make an effort to invest more energy, you may want to consider ending the relationship.

Know How to Navigate Disagreement in a Healthy Way

If you are working on adapting to being in a healthy relationship, the difference between *arguing* and *fighting* can be confusing. It is healthy and normal to have disagreements with your friend or loved one. However, there is a big difference between arguing and fighting.

When two people argue, they present their concerns and calmly discuss the feelings and issues related to those concerns. It is possible to talk about problems in a respectful way and without stirring up anger.

If you were in a toxic relationship, you most likely didn't feel safe bringing up concerns. And for a good reason—you were either told your needs weren't important, didn't matter, or worse yet, it turned into verbal or physical abuse. Now that you are turning the corner and healing, it's essential to know that avoiding an argument may seem like the best option for self-preservation, but it isn't. Research shows that when you have healthy relationships, talking about an issue and resolving it leads to a significant decrease in negative feelings compared to when you avoid talking about it.[1]

Of course, it feels easier (at least temporarily) to avoid arguments. But if you are with someone who is emotionally healthy, taking the risk of discussing an issue can pay off in the long term. If having healthy disagreements is difficult for you, try scheduling time for arguments in your relationship. It might sound silly or forced, but trust me—it works. It helps in two major ways. One, it prevents fights about those issues. And two, hot-button topics are saved for the scheduled argument time rather than brought up randomly when you might react in anger.

Have a set day and time where the two of you address an issue. Discuss one problem at a time, and each person alternates on choosing the topic. The scheduled argument should last no more than forty-five minutes; any longer than that, and the discussion can get out of hand.

The rules of scheduled arguments are as follows:

- No name-calling or personal attacks
- No bringing up the past
- No interrupting
- Stick to the topic at hand
- If either partner gets upset, they can step away for ten minutes

Each partner spends up to fifteen minutes giving their opinion about the topic. Then, take fifteen minutes to wrap up: you can agree to disagree, table the issue for another time, or decide to take action.

Surround Yourself with Healthy People

Chances are that from now on you will spot toxicity immediately. You already know what to look for, and those internal alarm bells will ring quickly. You know what an unhealthy person looks like—now, let's recap what a healthy person looks like. A healthy person

- Has boundaries
- Takes time to have fun
- Takes care of herself
- Finds ways to enrich her life
- Accepts setbacks as part of life and figures out what to do differently next time
- Takes things seriously when appropriate
- Understands that she and other people make mistakes
- Realizes that what other people do and think is not her responsibility
- Provides support to others but doesn't try to "fix" them or their situation
- Meets people where they are at, not where she would like them to be
- Knows what is and isn't under her control

You deserve to have healthy and supportive relationships. When you interact with an emotionally healthy person, you tend to feel more confident and comfortable. People's attitudes and emotions are contagious, so choose the people in your life with care.[2] Reach out to others in your life who are healthy, or try to meet new ones—revisit Chapter 8 for ideas.

• • • • •

In this chapter, you learned how to avoid a toxic relationship in the future: remember the key signs of toxicity and the importance of protecting yourself from unhealthy dynamics. We explored how to set the foundations for healthy relationships, including being aware of your attachment style, looking at new people with clear eyes, making a list of your criteria, and determining the right time to be vulnerable. We covered codependent behavior and how to break that pattern in the future. And we learned that disagreement is a natural and important part of every relationship—and how to do it in a healthy way. It may take some time to get used to building healthy relationships, but surrounding yourself with people who treat others with kindness and respect will create more time and peace in your life. I believe you can do it—and it will be so worth it.

YOU WILL HEAL

DECIDING TO LEAVE A TOXIC SITUATION CAN BE VERY DIFFICULT, AND healing is a journey that takes time. As you learned from the stories throughout this book, however, you aren't alone on that journey. And, as these examples show, a happier, calmer, and healthier life is within anyone's reach.

• • • • •

Remember Aya from Chapter 2? She didn't respond to her friend Enzo's text. She felt violated—first by how her ex, Lou, had treated her throughout their relationship, and then how he had apparently sent Enzo as a flying monkey to get her back. Neither Enzo nor Lou needed to know anything about how she was doing or whether she was going to come back. After cutting off all contact, she was finally able to sleep without waking up in the middle of the night with anxiety. That's not to say she was feeling relieved most of the time—she was still angry, disappointed, and sad. But over time, Aya started reconnecting with the friends and family she'd been distanced from in her marriage. She also started going to therapy to talk, not only about the anger she had toward Lou, but also the anger she had toward herself for staying so long. Aya was making progress toward forgiving herself, and she noticed that healthier people were appearing in her life. She felt a little better every day.

• • • • •

Hasim, whom you met in the introduction, decided his best course of action was to put in his two-weeks' notice, even though he didn't have another job lined up. He realized that staying at a toxic work environment was causing damage—not only to him, but also to his relationships with his family and friends because he constantly felt so angry and on edge. After Hasim's last day of work, he had his first sound night of sleep in weeks. His family and friends have commented that it seems as if he is back to feeling like himself again. Hasim is currently consulting an attorney to see whether his employer violated any laws. He's also working with a career counselor to process what happened and figure out how he should talk about his previous job in interviews. Hasim has already had several interviews for a new job, and he is looking forward to having a new start. But most of all, he feels more present in his other relationships because work stress isn't occupying his mind.

• • • • •

Tammy and Isaac from Chapter 3 finally did come to an agreement about the amount of money he would pay her for her half of the business. Once the divorce agreement was signed, Tammy felt relieved and deeply saddened. She didn't expect to feel such a sense of loss—she knew that she would never hear from Isaac again. There was no reason for them to speak with each other, except to do the personal and business taxes for that year, and afterward, if there were big events in their kids' lives. Tammy was surprised to find that she missed hearing from Isaac, even after all she felt that he had put her through. In therapy, she came to terms with the fact that it wasn't really Isaac she missed; she just missed having someone there. But Isaac hadn't even really been present in their marriage for years. Tammy's biggest breakthrough was realizing that she had already been on her own for a long time—and she had the skills and strength to get through it. Tapping into the resilience that she had always had helped Tammy rebuild her life. Now, she is dating again and has met someone who gets along well with her kids. He's been kind and considerate and she can see a future with him. But even if it doesn't work out, Tammy knows she'll be okay.

• • • • •

There is a tremendous amount of power in the ability to walk away from people or places that aren't healthy for you. Walking away can be painful, but it's not nearly as painful as staying longer in a toxic situation where you are compromising your values and self-worth. Aya, Hasim, and Tammy took courageous steps to be free from abusive relationships or situations—and if you've been following along with the recommendations and journal prompts in this book, so have you.

Look at how far you've come since taking those first steps to leave:

- You picked up this book because you've dealt with a toxic person in a relationship, in a friendship, in your family, or in your workplace. In Chapter 1, you identified what made this relationship toxic, why you might have gotten into it, and why you stayed.
- Going "no contact" with a toxic person is usually the best way to remove her unhealthy influence from your life, and in Chapter 2 you put necessary distance between yourself and the toxic person. If no contact was not an option, such as in coparenting or continued professional relationships, then low contact was the next best thing.
- Although you may be wanting closure from the toxic person to move on in your life, you may not receive it from him. In Chapter 3, you found your closure, perhaps through journaling, practicing good self-care, or writing an unsent letter—or maybe you realized you don't need to get closure to have a good life.
- You may have been angry at yourself for not leaving the relationship sooner or for not having as much contact with trusted family and friends. In Chapter 4, you saw how no one is immune from toxic people, and you began to let go of this anger and forgive yourself.

- In Chapter 5, you reestablished boundaries, letting people know your limits so you can have healthy interactions and build confidence within yourself. Now, you say no to activities or people who drain your energy, insist on being spoken to with respect, and are okay changing your mind when something doesn't feel right to you.

- You might find therapy helpful throughout your journey. After reading Chapter 6, I hope that you met with a mental health professional (MHP) (though it's okay if you need to speak with a few MHPs before you find a good "fit").

- Practicing self-care is essential at any time, but especially after leaving a toxic situation when you may not have prioritized it. With the suggested practices in Chapter 7, you dedicated time every day to nurturing yourself.

- You may have been isolated from family and friends when you were around the toxic person. (Your family may have even been toxic.) In Chapter 8, you reached out to the supportive and healthy people you care about, or you found a new support group. They've helped you get back to feeling like yourself again.

- In Chapter 9, you learned that the only way to work through grief is to experience it. It has likely been painful, and you may even feel out of control sometimes. Be reassured that feelings of grief do lessen over time. You will be okay.

- When we reach out to others in need, it takes our mind off our current experiences and helps us build new relationships and memories. In Chapter 10, you learned how volunteering helps you connect with your community. When you are ready, you may consider volunteering as an advocate for others who have experienced toxic situations.

- Finally, in Chapter 11, you began to navigate your new normal as you built relationships with others—avoiding the codependent dynamics you may be prone to, having realistic expectations, and knowing when the time is right to be vulnerable. You have a lifetime of healthy relationships ahead of you even if you have experienced toxic ones in the past.

Throughout this book, some suggestions or techniques may have seemed more accessible than others, and that is entirely okay. You can always return to challenging ones and work on them later. Or you might decide that a recommendation is just not for you. Anytime you work on healing yourself, whether through reconnecting with others, volunteering your time, or attending counseling sessions, time is well spent.

Before you close this book, I want to leave you with some last recommendations.

First, if you've kept a journal along the way, revisit what you wrote, drew, painted, or created. Journaling helps you process your experiences, and revisiting your earlier entries can show you just how much progress you've made. You may discover you now have healthier relationships, not only with healthier people, but also with yourself. If you haven't yet begun journaling, now's the time to start!

Second, though I have said it many times throughout this book, I'll say it once again: reach out to a mental health professional who can help you sort through the trauma you've experienced. Your pain is real and you deserve resolution. You may find that therapy not only helps you deal with feelings of anger toward the person or persons that hurt you but also helps you with anger you might be feeling toward yourself.

Third, always remember that there is no "finish line" to healing from toxic people and situations, and progress doesn't happen in a straight line. It's more like a jagged peak—you may start having more good days than bad days, and then the bad days seem less bad. You may have a day when you feel like you've slid backward in your progress. I have worked with many clients who were able to heal from trauma they have experienced and they go on to have happy, productive, and meaningful lives, surrounded by emotionally healthy people. I wish I could speed up the healing process for you, but it just takes time and some introspective work. Remember, you are still making progress, even if it doesn't always feel like it. You can always reread this book and revisit the activities and prompts to continue your journey.

If you take just one thing with you from this book, I hope it is this: Know that you can heal from an abusive relationship or situation. There is hope. The road ahead of you may be a rocky one, but things can and do get better. You will be okay. You will heal. You will thrive.

ACKNOWLEDGMENTS

Thank you to my clients, who were gracious in lending their stories for this book. Thank you to my editor, Claire Schulz; editorial director, Renée Sedliar; and my agent, Carol Mann. Thank you to everyone at Hachette Go for making this book possible. Thank you to family and friends—Bill Moulton; Claude Moulton, Esq.; Christine Whitney, Esq.; R. Michael Sitz; Scamp Moulton; Valerie Theng Matherne, Esq.; Ari Tuckman, PsyD; Roberto Olivardia, PhD; and Mark Bertin, MD. Your support and encouragement mean the world to me.

RESOURCES

Anger

Albert Ellis. *How to Control Your Anger Before It Controls You.* New York: Citadel, 2016.

Harriet Lerner. *The Dance of Anger: A Woman's Guide to Changing the Patterns of Intimate Relationships.* New York: William Morrow, 2014.

Attachment Styles

Annie Chen. *The Attachment Theory Workbook: Powerful Tools to Promote Understanding, Increase Stability, and Build Lasting Relationships.* Emeryville, CA: Althea Press, 2019.

Diane Heller. *The Power of Attachment: How to Create Deep and Lasting Intimate Relationships.* Louisville, CO: Sounds True, 2019.

Amir Levine and Rachel Heller. *Attached: The New Science of Adult Attachment and How It Can Help You Find—and Keep—Love.* New York: TarcherPerigee, 2012.

Attorneys

American Bar Association
www.americanbar.com

Boundaries

Robert Alberti and Michael Emmons. *Your Perfect Right: Assertiveness and Equality in Your Life and Relationships,* 10th ed. Oakland, CA: Impact, 2017.

Shandelle Hether-Gray. *Assertiveness Workbook: Practical Exercises to Improve Communication, Set Boundaries, and Be Your Best Advocate.* Emeryville, CA: Rockridge Press, 2020.

Lisa M. Schab. *Cool, Calm, and Confident: A Workbook to Help Kids Learn Assertiveness Skills.* Oakland, CA: Instant Help, 2009.

Codependency

Melody Beattie. *Codependent No More Workbook.* Center City, MN: Hazelden, 2011.

Krystal Mazzola. *The Codependency Workbook: Simple Practices for Developing and Maintaining Your Independence.* Emeryville, CA: Rockridge Press, 2020.

Coparenting

Margalis Fjelstad and Jean McBride. *Raising Resilient Children with a Borderline or Narcissistic Parent.* Washington, DC: Rowman & Littlefield Publishers, 2020.

Jeremy S. Gaies and James B. Morris. *Mindful Coparenting: A Child-Friendly Path Through Divorce.* CreateSpace Independent Publishing Platform, 2014.

Carl Knickerbocker. *The Parallel Parenting Solution: Eliminate Conflict with Your Ex, Create the Life You Want.* Independent Publishing Corporation, 2021.

2 Houses
www.2houses.com

CoParenter
www.coparenter.com

CoParently
www.coparently.com

Our Family Wizard
www.ourfamilywizard.com

Talking Parents
www.talkingparents.com

We Parent
www.weparent.app

Domestic Violence

DomesticShelters.org
www.domesticshelters.org

National Coalition Against Domestic Violence
www.ncadv.org
303-839-1852

National Domestic Violence Hotline
www.thehotline.org
1-800-799-SAFE (7233)

Victim Connect Resource Center
www.victimconnect.org
1-855-4VICTIM (855-484-2846)

Family Law Attorneys

Family Law Organization
www.familylaw.org
(for pro bono services, see Pro Bono Legal Services, page 223)

Gaslighting

Amy Marlow-McCoy. *The Gaslighting Recovery Workbook: Healing from Emotional Abuse.* Emeryville, CA: Rockridge Press, 2020.

Stephanie Sarkis. *Gaslighting: Recognize Manipulative and Emotionally Abusive People—and Break Free.* New York: Da Capo Press, 2018.

Grief

Pema Chödrön. *When Things Fall Apart: Heart Advice for Difficult Times.* Boulder, CO: Shambhala Publications, 2016.

Melba Colgrove, Harold H. Bloomfield, and Peter McWilliams. *How to Survive the Loss of a Love.* Los Angeles: Prelude Press, 2006.

John W. James and Russell Friedman. *The Grief Recovery Handbook: The Action Program for Moving Beyond Death, Divorce, and Other Losses.* New York: Harper Perennial, 2009.

Elisabeth Kübler-Ross. *On Grief and Grieving: Finding the Meaning of Grief Through the Five Stages of Loss.* New York: Scribner, 2014.

Harold S. Kushner. *When Bad Things Happen to Good People.* New York: Anchor Books, 2004.

C. S. Lewis. *A Grief Observed.* New York: HarperCollins Publishers, 2001.

Thich Nhat Hanh. *No Mud, No Lotus: The Art of Transforming Suffering.* Berkeley, CA: Parallax Press, 2014.

Meditation and Mindfulness

Matthew Sockolov. *Practicing Mindfulness: 75 Essential Meditations to Reduce Stress, Improve Mental Health, and Find Peace in the Everyday.* Emeryville, CA: Althea Press, 2018.

Buddhify
www.buddhify.com

Calm
www.calm.com

Headspace
www.headspace.com

Inner Health Studio
www.innerhealthstudio.com

Mindful
www.mindful.org

MyLife
www.my.life

Stop, Breathe, and Think
www.stopbreathethink.com

Ten Percent Happier
www.tenpercent.com

Mental Health Professionals and Therapy

American Association for Marriage and Family Therapy
www.aamft.org

American Association of Sexuality Educators, Counselors, and Therapists
www.aasect.org

American Psychological Association
www.apa.org

Association for Play Therapy
www.a4pt.org

GoodTherapy
www.goodtherapy.org

National Board for Certified Counselors
www.nbcc.org

Psychology Today Directory
psychologytoday.com/us/therapists
psychologytoday.com/us/types-of-therapy

Narcissism

Shahida Arabi. *The Highly Sensitive Person's Guide to Dealing with Toxic People: How to Reclaim Your Power from Narcissists and Other Manipulators.* Oakland, CA: New Harbinger Publications, 2020.

Joseph Burgo. *The Narcissist You Know: Defending Yourself Against Extreme Narcissists in an All-About-Me Age.* New York: Touchstone, 2015.

Ramani Durvasula. *Should I Stay or Should I Go? Surviving a Relationship with a Narcissist.* New York: Post Hill Press, 2017.

Bill Eddy and L. Georgi DiStefano. *It's All Your Fault at Work: Managing Narcissists and Other High-Conflict People.* Scottsdale, AZ: Unhooked Books, 2015.

Bill Eddy and Randi Kreger. *Splitting: Protecting Yourself While Divorcing Someone with Borderline or Narcissistic Personality Disorder.* Oakland, CA: New Harbinger Publications, 2021.

Paul T. Mason and Randi Kreger. *Stop Walking on Eggshells: Taking Your Life Back When Someone You Care About Has Borderline Personality Disorder.* Oakland, CA: New Harbinger Publications, 2020.

Kimberlee Roth and Freda B. Friedman. *Surviving a Borderline Parent: How to Heal Your Childhood Wounds and Build Trust, Boundaries, and Self-Esteem.* Oakland, CA: New Harbinger Publications, 2004.

Pro Bono Legal Services

Administration for Community Living—independent living for older adults and people with disabilities
www.acl.gov

LawHelp.org
www.lawhelp.org

Legal Services Corporation
www.lsc.gov

Self-Care

Robyn L. Gobin. *The Self-Care Prescription: Powerful Solutions to Manage Stress, Reduce Anxiety, and Increase Well-Being.* Emeryville, CA: Althea Press, 2019.

Zoe Shaw. *A Year of Self-Care: Daily Practices and Inspiration for Caring for Yourself.* Emeryville, CA: Rockridge Press, 2021.

Self-Compassion

Christopher K. Germer. *The Mindful Path to Self-Compassion: Freeing Yourself from Destructive Thoughts and Emotions.* New York: Guilford Press, 2009.

Joy Johnson. *The Self-Compassion Workbook: Practical Exercises to Approach Your Thoughts, Emotions, and Actions with Kindness.* Emeryville, CA: Rockridge Press, 2020.

William Martin. *The Tao of Forgiveness: The Healing Power of Forgiving Others and Yourself.* New York: TarcherPerigee, 2010.

Sexual Assault

Rape, Abuse & Incest National Network, National Sexual Assault Hotline
www.rainn.org
1-800-656-HOPE (4673)

Suicide Prevention
National Suicide Prevention Lifeline
www.suicidepreventionlifeline.org
1-800-273-8255

Support Groups
Adult Children of Alcoholics & Dysfunctional Families
www.adultchildren.org

Al-Anon
www.al-anon.org

Codependents Anonymous
www.coda.org

Volunteering and Volunteer Organizations
Matthieu Ricard. *Altruism: The Power of Compassion to Change Yourself and the World.* New York: Little, Brown and Company, 2015.

Charity Watch
www.charitywatch.org

Global Volunteers
www.globalvolunteers.org

US Natural and Cultural Resources Volunteer Portal
www.volunteer.gov

Volunteer Match
www.volunteermatch.org

Workplace Harassment
Adrienne Lawrence. *Staying in the Game: The Playbook for Beating Workplace Sexual Harassment.* New York: TarcherPerigee, 2021.
Robert I. Sutton. *The No Asshole Rule: Building a Civilized Workplace and Surviving One That Isn't.* New York: Business Plus, 2010.

US Equal Employment Opportunity Commission (EEOC)
www.eeoc.gov/harassment

GLOSSARY

Acceptance and commitment therapy (ACT). A type of cognitive-behavioral therapy in which you learn to decrease your emotional connection to your thoughts through a practice known as cognitive defusion or deliteralization. This method helps you to recognize your thoughts for what they are—just thoughts—to lessen their power over you and help you cope with uncomfortable thoughts and feelings. To work through your emotions, you need to experience them rather than ignore them or find a distraction from them. *Mindfulness meditation* is one facet of ACT.

Attachment style. The particular way in which you relate to other people in relationships. Your attachment style is formed in childhood depending on how your caregivers interacted with you. There are four main attachment styles—anxious, avoidant, disorganized, and secure. The anxious, avoidant, and disorganized attachment styles are known as insecure attachments.

Boundaries. Healthy guidelines or limits that you place on yourself and your relationships. Toxic people may continually violate your boundaries. Types of boundaries include emotional, physical, sexual, time, and mental.

Codependency. An unhealthy reliance—mental, emotional, or physical—on a romantic partner, friend, or family member. You feel responsible for other people's feelings or problems. You may depend too much on your partner or other people in your life for emotional stability, validation, or a sense of purpose. You may be covering or making excuses for a person's addictive or abusive behavior.

Coercive control. A term used to describe abuse that has the intent of harming, punishing, or frightening a person. It includes threats, intimidation, humiliation, and assault. In the United Kingdom, coercive control is a criminal offense.

Cognitive-behavioral therapy (CBT). A type of talk therapy that focuses, in part, on recognizing and changing thinking distortions (faulty inner dialogue). When inner dialogue changes, your behavior toward yourself and others changes.

Cognitive defusion. The practice of detaching from one's thoughts and emotions to reduce distress. It is a technique used in *acceptance and commitment therapy*. Practicing cognitive defusion can help people view their thoughts and feelings as just that—not as absolute truth or commands. One cognitive defusion technique is acknowledging a thought and rephrasing it as "I notice I'm having the thought that . . ."

Cognitive dissonance. When you receive information that contradicts your beliefs and doesn't fit with what you know about people and the world around you. Experiencing cognitive dissonance can lead to feelings of confusion, anxiety, and depression.

Cognitive empathy. When a toxic person appears to be showing empathy toward you, but there are no emotions behind his words. A toxic person will say what he thinks is the "right" thing to make you feel as if he cares.

Compassion fatigue. The physical, emotional, and psychological impact of helping other people, especially through difficult times, that drains your ability to empathize. Also known as secondary traumatic stress. If you are working with people who have been traumatized, you may experience a heightened level of stress and a marked change in how you perceive others. You may experience burnout, including feelings of exhaustion.

Couples Therapy. A form of talk therapy where partners meet together with a mental health professional to discuss current and past issues in their relationship. The therapist may also have one individual session with each partner at the beginning of treatment.

Devaluing. Part of a toxic person's idealizing-devaluing-discarding process. Devaluing occurs when a toxic person treats you as if you aren't valuable or important. Criticism increases, and you are blamed for things that aren't your fault.

Dialectical behavior therapy (DBT). A type of cognitive-behavioral therapy in which the goals are improving stress tolerance, keeping emotions in check, and finding a balance between acceptance and change. Through DBT, you come to recognize that feeling competing emotions is a normal and common part of the human experience.

Discarding. Part of a toxic person's idealizing-devaluing-discarding process. Discarding occurs when the toxic person ends the relationship or "ghosts" you because she has found new *narcissistic supply* or you aren't fulfilling her unrealistic expectations. You are almost always blamed for the discard. Often preceded by *narcissistic rage.*

Economic abuse. A form of domestic violence where the abuser prevents access to economic resources, and the victim is forced to rely on the abuser for financial needs. Forms of economic abuse include forcing the victim to surrender their financial accounts and assets and forcing the victim to quit their job.

Ego-dystonic personality. *Ego-dystonic* refers to having thoughts and feelings that are in conflict with your self-image. While on the surface, that may sound like a bad thing, having that personality or mind-set means that you can recognize when a behavior isn't working well for you, and you can seek help to correct it. Healthy people tend to have *ego-dystonic* personalities. See *ego-syntonic personality.*

Ego-syntonic personality. *Ego-syntonic* refers to having thoughts and feelings that are in harmony with your self-image, values, and ways of thinking. A person with this personality or mind-set believes he is fine psychologically, that his perceptions and behaviors are reasonable, and that his behavior should be acceptable to others. Found in personality disorders, such as *narcissistic personality disorder* (NPD). See *ego-dystonic personality.*

Emotional ammunition. When a toxic person gathers information about your vulnerabilities to use them against you in the future, she is said to be collecting emotional ammunition.

Emotional blackmail. A type of manipulation where a toxic person uses guilt, shame, or threats to control you. You may also be told you are obligated to fulfill the toxic person's needs. One example of emotional blackmail is when you tell your partner you are ending the relationship and he tells you he is going to harm himself if you go.

Emotional intimacy. A deep and caring connection with a person in which both of you are free to be authentic and share your thoughts and feelings without judgment. A toxic person may engage in *trauma dumping, cognitive empathy,* and *love-bombing* to artificially create emotional intimacy. True emotional intimacy develops gradually and can't be forced.

Enabling. Supporting a person's harmful and toxic behaviors. Enabling includes minimizing a person's issues, lying or making excuses for his behavior, and/or working harder than he is at changing his toxic behavior.

External locus of control. Your mood changes based on what happens around you. If you are in a bad mood, it is difficult for you to take yourself out of it. In contrast, when you have an internal locus of control, you feel solid and grounded. See also *internal locus of control.*

Family therapy. A form of talk therapy where members of a family meet with a mental health professional to discuss issues regarding the dynamics of the family. Family members may be asked to share their experiences and provide feedback.

Flying monkey. A person who carries messages to you from a toxic person. A flying monkey may or may not be aware of the toxicity of that person. Named after the Wicked Witch of the West's messengers in *The Wizard of Oz.*

Future faking. A toxic person promises you the future you have wanted as a way to get you back into a relationship with him. Once you have reestablished a relationship, the toxic person doesn't follow through with what they had promised and may even deny they said it.

Gaslighting. A form of psychological and emotional abuse. It is a series of manipulation techniques in which an abuser makes a victim question his reality. Over time, the victim feels as if he is losing his mind and that he cannot trust his own perception of the world.

Grounding technique. A coping strategy or practice that helps a person immediately refocus on the present moment when experiencing flashbacks, dissociation, anxiety, or panic. It is a practice that can be done at any time or location.

Group therapy. A form of therapy where a mental health professional leads a group of individuals who have issues in common. Part of healing in group therapy is due to universality—the knowledge that others have experienced similar feelings and events.

Hoovering. When a toxic person tries to lure you back into contact with him, possibly with the intent of sucking you back into a relationship. Contact can range from sending you a one-word text to showing up at your residence. They may promise you that things will be better between you. This behavior is named after the vacuum cleaner brand. See *future faking.*

Hypervigilance. Being on high alert as a consequence of being in a toxic relationship or situation. You may have a strong startle reflex and you default to being on the lookout for danger. It can be a symptom of post-traumatic stress disorder (PTSD).

Idealizing. Part of a toxic person's idealizing-devaluing-discarding process. A toxic person will treat you like you can do no wrong at the beginning of a relationship. They treat you as if you are a magical special creature. But it doesn't last. See *love-bombing.*

Individual therapy. A form of talk therapy where a person meets one-on-one with a mental health professional to discuss current and past issues. Individual therapy can be attended either in person or via telehealth. Family-of-origin experiences may be addressed to help process and understand current behavior.

Intermittent reinforcement. Positive reinforcement is given for some, but not all, occurrences of a behavior. There is a random order to this reinforcement, causing a person to repeat the behavior more often than if they were given continuous positive reinforcement. This may result in addictive behavior. An abuser may be affectionate at unpredictable times, intensifying the trauma bond.

Internal locus of control. Your mood is fairly stable regardless of what happens around you. You feel that you can handle most things because you look inward to find strength and resilience. See also *external locus of control.*

Living or ambiguous loss. Someone who a person is grieving over is continually present in that person's life, such as ending a relationship with a coparent. There is a lack of finality to the loss, and a person may continually feel the sense of loss.

Love-bombing. Part of a toxic person's idealizing behaviors at the beginning of a relationship. The person showers you with affection and/or gifts to rush you into commitment. Once you are in the relationship, the love-bombing stops and *devaluing* begins.

Maladaptive coping. Engaging in high-risk behaviors to feel something other than anger or sadness. A common occurrence after ending a toxic relationship or leaving a toxic situation. Includes increased alcohol or drug use, engaging in high-risk sexual behavior, and undereating or overeating.

Mindfulness meditation. A type of meditation where you focus on what you are sensing and feeling in the moment. Techniques include focusing on breathing and being active while you focus on the present.

Narcissism. Self-involvement and a sense of entitlement, to the degree that others' needs aren't considered. A person that is a narcissist may or may not qualify for a diagnosis of *narcissistic personality disorder (NPD).*

Narcissistic injury. An event that threatens a narcissist's ego. It could be triggered by a person enforcing a healthy boundary or anything the narcissist perceives as "disloyal." A narcissist may respond with *narcissistic rage* or *stonewalling.*

Narcissistic personality disorder (NPD). A cluster of symptoms that impact a person's day-to-day functioning and ability to form healthy relationships. Symptoms include believing she is entitled to "special" treatment, exploiting others, lacking empathy, and expectations that she will be treated as superior to others. A person with NPD tends to have an *ego-syntonic* personality.

Narcissistic rage. When someone sets boundaries with a toxic person or challenges him, resulting in a *narcissistic injury*, he may respond by flying into a rage. The onset of narcissistic rage can be instantaneous, with no warning signs. The toxic person may then act the next day as if the narcissistic rage never happened.

Narcissistic supply. A narcissist needs constant attention from others, and the source of that attention is her supply. When the newness of a relationship wears off or if she feels someone has been disloyal to her, she may move on to new supply. It is common for a narcissist to have more than one narcissistic supply while she claims she is monogamous, and she may keep her exes in rotation for easy supply.

Object constancy. The ability to believe that a relationship remains stable even during conflicts or difficulties. A toxic person has difficulty maintaining a concept of object constancy. Any conflict is seen as a threat to his ego and may result in *discarding* or *stonewalling*.

Reactive abuse. When you fight back against an abuser as a form of survival and self-preservation. It doesn't mean you are abusive—however, a toxic person may try to convince you that you are the "real" abuser.

Shaping a behavior. A process for establishing a behavior. A person works toward the desired behavior by reinforcing any behaviors that approximate the desired behavior. A person who has a goal of going to bed an hour earlier gives themselves positive reinforcement for going to bed fifteen minutes earlier each night, then thirty minutes earlier, and so on.

Sociopath. A person who knows right from wrong but just doesn't care. He typically exploits people and has little or no feelings of empathy.

Solution-focused therapy. A type of talk therapy that includes defining your strengths and learning methods to direct your energy to heal yourself. One of the concepts of solution-focused therapy is that when you change just one thing in your life for the better, it results in many benefits.

Stockholm syndrome. An emotional response in which a victim of abuse or a hostage develops an emotional attachment to or identification with her abuser or captor. Named after a case in Stockholm where hostages not only sympathized with their captors but also refused to testify against them and raised money for their legal defense. Stockholm syndrome is a type of *trauma bonding*.

Stonewalling. A form of emotional abuse where a toxic person punishes someone with the use of silent treatment. It usually occurs as a response to the enforcement of healthy boundaries, or when a toxic person perceives someone as being disloyal.

Sunk cost effect. Our tendency to continue to pursue something (a relationship or other endeavor) after we've invested time, effort, or money in it—even when the endeavor isn't working out. We are less likely to leave a toxic relationship when we feel we have invested time and effort into making it work. We want to feel that everything we gave up to make the relationship work was worth it and that we didn't "waste time." However, spending more time with a toxic person increases a feeling of wasted time and effort.

Trauma bonding. When a survivor of abuse develops an attachment to or sympathy toward her abuser. Trauma bonding can occur in any interaction where a person is abused, including in domestic violence, child abuse, human trafficking, cults, and hostage situations. *Stockholm syndrome* is a type of trauma bonding.

Trauma dump. When a toxic person tells you too much of their history of trauma soon after meeting you. It may be indicative of a lack of boundaries or may be used as a way to lure you into a relationship. It is also used as a way to artificially create *emotional intimacy.*

Triangulation. Pitting two people against each other so they have conflict and a strained relationship. For instance, a toxic person might falsely tell a victim that her sister said something mean about her, and that she has "a right to know." It is one of the ways a toxic person works to isolate a victim from her friends and family. It is also a way that a toxic person tries to take the focus off his abusive behavior.

Vicarious traumatization. When hearing about others' traumatic experiences causes you to experience symptoms of anxiety, depression, and burnout. You may also relive aspects of your own trauma.

NOTES

Chapter 1

1. Joan Reid et al., "Trauma Bonding and Interpersonal Violence," in *Psychology of Trauma*, ed. Thijs van Leeuwen and Marieke Brouwer (Hauppage, NY: Nova Science Publishers, 2013).

2. Matthew H. Logan, "Stockholm Syndrome: Held Hostage by the One You Love," *Violence and Gender* 5, no. 2 (2018): 67–69, http://doi.org:10.1089/vio.2017.0076.

3. Sara Rego, Joana Arntes, and Paula Magalhães, "Is There a Sunk Cost Effect in Committed Relationships?," *Current Psychology* 37, no. 3 (2018): 508–519, http://doi.org:10.1007/s12144-016-9529-9.

Chapter 2

1. Zoe Rejaän, Inge E. van der Valk, and Susan Branje, "Postdivorce Coparenting Patterns and Relations with Adolescent Adjustment," *Journal of Family Issues* (2021), http://doi.org:10.1177/0192513X211030027.

2. Linda Nielsen, "Re-examining the Research on Parental Conflict, Coparenting, and Custody Arrangements," *Psychology, Public Policy, and Law* 23, no. 2 (2017): 211, http://doi.org:10.1037/law0000109.

3. Sara Gale et al., "The Impact of Workplace Harassment on Health in a Working Cohort," *Frontiers in Psychology* 10 (2019): 1181, http://doi.org:10.3389/fpsyg.2019.01181; Shazia Nauman, Sania Zahra Malik, and Faryal Jalil, "How Workplace Bullying Jeopardizes Employees' Life Satisfaction: The Roles of Job Anxiety and Insomnia," *Frontiers in Psychology* 10 (2019): 2292, http://doi.org:10.3389/fpsyg.2019.02292.

Chapter 3

1. Marnin J. Heisel and Gordon L. Flett, "Do Meaning in Life and Purpose in Life Protect Against Suicide Ideation Among Community-Residing Older Adults?," in *Meaning in Positive and Existential Psychology*, ed. Alexander Batthyany and Pninit Russo-Netzer (New York: Springer, 2014), 303–324.

2. Matthew Evans, "A Future Without Forgiveness: Beyond Reconciliation in Transitional Justice," *International Politics* 55, no. 5 (2018): 678–692.

3. Karina Schumann and Gregory M. Walton, "Rehumanizing the Self After Victimization: The Roles of Forgiveness Versus Revenge," *Journal of Personality and Social Psychology* (2021), http://doi.org:10.1037/pspi0000367.

4. LaVelle Hendricks et al., "The Effects of Anger on the Brain and Body," *National Forum Journal of Counseling and Addiction* 2, no. 1 (2013): 1–12, http://www.national forum.com/Electronic%20Journal%20Volumes/Hendricks,%20LaVelle%20The%20 Effects%20of%20Anger%20on%20the%20Brain%20and%20Body%20NFJCA%20 V2%20N1%202013.pdf.

Chapter 4

1. Diana-Mirela Cândea and Aurora Szentagotai-Tătar, "Shame-Proneness, Guilt-Proneness and Anxiety Symptoms: A Meta-analysis," *Journal of Anxiety Disorders* 58 (2018): 78–106, http://doi.org:10.1016/j.janxdis.2018.07.005; Malgorzata Gambin and Carla Sharp, "The Relations Between Empathy, Guilt, Shame and Depression in Inpatient Adolescents," *Journal of Affective Disorders* 241 (2018): 381–387, http://doi.org:10.1016/j.jad.2018.08.068.

Chapter 5

1. Shanhong Luo, "Effects of Texting on Satisfaction in Romantic Relationships: The Role of Attachment," *Computers in Human Behavior* 33 (2014): 145–152, http://doi.org:10.1016/j.chb.2014.01.014.

2. Luo, "Effects of Texting on Satisfaction in Romantic Relationships."

3. Shanhong Luo and Shelley Tuney, "Can Texting Be Used to Improve Romantic Relationships?—The Effects of Sending Positive Text Messages on Relationship Satisfaction," *Computers in Human Behavior* 49 (2015): 670–678, http://doi.org:10.1016/j.chb.2014.11.035.

4. Laurel A. Milam et al., "The Relationship Between Self-Efficacy and Well-Being Among Surgical Residents," *Journal of Surgical Education* 76, no. 2 (2019): 321–328, http://doi.org:10.1016/j.jsurg.2018.07.028; Ulrich Orth, Ruth Yasemin Erol, and Eva C. Luciano, "Development of Self-Esteem from Age 4 to 94 Years: A Meta-analysis of Longitudinal Studies," *Psychological Bulletin* 144, no. 10 (2018): 1045–1080, http://doi.org:10.1037/bul0000161.

5. Zahra Mirbolook Jalali, Azadeh Farghadani, and Maryam Ejlali-Vardoogh, "Effect of Cognitive-Behavioral Training on Pain Self-Efficacy, Self-Discovery, and Perception in Patients with Chronic Low-Back Pain: A Quasi-Experimental Study," *Anesthesiology and Pain Medicine* 9, no. 2 (2019): e78905, http://doi.org:10.5812/aapm.78905.

6. Edward Kruk, "Parental Alienation as a Form of Emotional Child Abuse: Current State of Knowledge and Future Directions for Research," *Family Science Review* 22 no. 4 (2018): 141–164; Wilfrid von Boch-Galhau, "Parental Alienation (Syndrome)—A Serious Form of Child Psychological Abuse," *Mental Health and Family Medicine* 14 (2018): 725–739.

Chapter 7

1. Hyon Joo Hong et al., "Correlations Between Stress, Depression, Body Mass Index, and Food Addiction Among Korean Nursing Students," *Journal of Addictions Nursing* 31, no. 4 (2020): 236–242, http://doi.org:10.1097/JAN.0000000000000362.

2. Kathleen Mikkelsen et al., "Exercise and Mental Health," *Maturitas* 106 (2017): 48–56, http://doi.org:10.1016/j.maturitas.2017.09.003.

3. Shadab A. Rahman et al., "Characterizing the Temporal Dynamics of Melatonin and Cortisol Changes in Response to Nocturnal Light Exposure," *Scientific Reports* 9, no. 1 (2019): 19720, http://doi.org:10.1038/s41598-019-54806-7.

4. Rohan Nagare et al., "Nocturnal Melatonin Suppression by Adolescents and Adults for Different Levels, Spectra, and Durations of Light Exposure," *Journal of Biological Rhythms* 34, no. 2 (2019): 178–194, http://doi.org:10.1177/0748730419828056.

5. Ariel Shensa et al., "Social Media Use and Depression and Anxiety Symptoms: A Cluster Analysis," *American Journal of Health Behavior* 42, no. 2 (2018): 116–128, http://doi.org:10.5993/AJHB.42.2.11.

6. Rasan Burhanand Jalal Moradzadeh, "Neurotransmitter Dopamine (DA) and Its Role in the Development of Social Media Addiction," *Journal of Neurology & Neurophysiology* 11, no. 7 (2020): 507.

Chapter 8

1. Jon M. Taylor, *The Case (for and) Against Multi-Level Marketing*, Consumer Awareness Institute, 2011, https://www.ftc.gov/sites/default/files/documents/public_comments/trade-regulation-rule-disclosure-requirements-and-prohibitions-concerning-business-opportunities-ftc.r511993-00008%C2%A0/00008-57281.pdf.

2. Michael J. Rosenfeld, Reuben J. Thomas, and Sonia Hausen, "Disintermediating Your Friends: How Online Dating in the United States Displaces Other Ways of Meeting," *Proceedings of the National Academy of Sciences* 116, no. 36 (2019): 17753–17758, http://doi.org:10.1073/pnas.1908630116.

3. Nur Hafeeza Ahmad Pazil, "Face, Voice and Intimacy in Long-Distance Close Friendships," *International Journal of Asian Social Science* 8, no. 11 (2018): 938–947, http://doi.org:10.18488/journal.1.2018.811.938.947.

Chapter 9

1. S. E. Kakarala et al., "The Neurobiological Reward System in Prolonged Grief Disorder (PGD): A Systematic Review," *Psychiatry Research: Neuroimaging* 303 (2020): 111135, http://doi.org:10.1016/j.pscychresns.2020.111135.

2. Tina M. Mason, Cindy S. Tofthagen, and Harleah G. Buck, "Complicated Grief: Risk Factors, Protective Factors, and Interventions," *Journal of Social Work in End-of-Life & Palliative Care* 16, no. 2 (2020): 151–174, http://doi.org:10.1080/15524256.2020.1745726; Anna Parisi et al., "The Relationship Between Substance Misuse and Complicated Grief: A Systematic Review," *Journal of Substance Abuse Treatment* 103 (2019): 43–57, http://doi.org:10.1016/j.jsat.2019.05.012.

3. Jie Li, Jorge N. Tendeiro, and Margaret Stroebe, "Guilt in Bereavement: Its Relationship with Complicated Grief and Depression," *International Journal of Psychology* 54, no. 4 (2019): 454–461, http://doi.org:10.1002/ijop.12483; Satomi Nakajima, "Complicated Grief: Recent Developments in Diagnostic Criteria and Treatment," *Philosophical Transactions of the Royal Society B: Biological Sciences* 373, no. 1754 (2018): 20170273, http://doi.org:10.1098/rstb.2017.0273.

4. Nooshin Pordelan et al., "How Online Career Counseling Changes Career Development: A Life Design Paradigm," *Education and Information Technologies* 23, no. 6 (2018): 2655–2672, http://doi.org:10.1007/s10639-018-9735-1.

5. Zuleide M. Ignácio et al., "Physical Exercise and Neuroinflammation in Major Depressive Disorder," *Molecular Neurobiology* 56, no. 12 (2019): 8323–8235, http://doi.org:10.1007/s12035-019-01670-1.

6. Anne Richards, Jennifer C. Kanady, and Thomas C. Neylan, "Sleep Disturbance in PTSD and Other Anxiety-Related Disorders: An Updated Review of Clinical Features, Physiological Characteristics, and Psychological and Neurobiological Mechanisms," *Neuropsychopharmacology* 45, no. 1 (2020): 55–73, http://doi.org:10.1038/s41386-019-0486-5.

Chapter 10

1. Robab Jahedi and Reza Derakhshani, "The Relationship Between Empathy and Altruism with Resilience Among Soldiers," *Military Psychology* 10, no. 40 (2020): 57–65.

2. R. Horowitz, "Compassion Cultivation," in *The Art and Science of Physician Wellbeing*, ed. Laura Weiss Roberts and Mickey Trockel (New York: Springer International Publishing, 2019): 33–53.

3. Priyanka Samuel and Smita Pandey, "Life Satisfaction and Altruism Among Religious Leaders," *International Journal of Indian Psychology* 6, no. 1 (2018): 89–95, http://doi.org:10.25215/0601.031.

4. Yi Feng et al., "When Altruists Cannot Help: The Influence of Altruism on the Mental Health of University Students During the COVID-19 Pandemic," *Globalization and Health* 16, no. 1 (2020): 1–8, http://doi.org:10.1186/s12992-020-00587-y.

5. Jerf W. K. Yeung, Zhuoni Zhang, and Tae Yeun Kim, "Volunteering and Health Benefits in General Adults: Cumulative Effects and Forms," *BMC Public Health* 18, no. 1 (2017): 1–8, http://doi.org:10.1186/s12889-017-4561-8.

6. M. G. Monaci, L. Scacchi, and M. G. Monteu, "Self-Conception and Volunteering: The Mediational Role of Motivations," *BPA—Applied Psychology Bulletin (Bollettino Di Psicologia Applicata)* 285 (2019): 38–50.

7. Dana C. Branson, "Vicarious Trauma, Themes in Research, and Terminology: A Review of Literature," *Traumatology* 25, no. 1 (2019): 2, http://doi.org:10.1037/trm0000161.

Chapter 11

1. Dakota D. Witzel and Robert S. Stawski, "Resolution Status and Age as Moderators for Interpersonal Everyday Stress and Stressor-Related Affect," *Journals of Gerontology: Series B* (2021): gbab006, http://doi.org:10.1093/geronb/gbab006.

2. Laura Petitta and Lixin Jiang, "How Emotional Contagion Relates to Burnout: A Moderated Mediation Model of Job Insecurity and Group Member Prototypicality," *International Journal of Stress Management* 27, no. 1 (2020): 12–22, http://doi.org:10.1037/str0000134.

INDEX